*To Maria*

# ONE FOR THE BOOK

# SON

## A LIFELONG JOURNEY OF AMAZING COINCIDENCES

# NICK TERRY

*Many Thanks*

*Nick Terry x*

Cover art by Spiffing Books
Edited by Richard Sheehan
Layout by Oliver Tooley
Printed in the UK by Short Run Press
Published by Blue Poppy Publishing, Devon

First Edition - Limited Print Run Hardcover

ISBN : 978-1-911438-92-2

## Thanks:

I would like to thank the following people for their, assistance, encouragement, invaluable help, and above all their patience and belief in me.

Aaron, Cathryn, Denver, Lisa & Val.

With Special Thanks to my new best friend - Simon

Dedicated

To Dad

Diane & Bailey

# Introduction

I've always had the feeling life has a plan for me. From the day I was born things have happened that make no logical sense. Of course, when I was young I didn't know that. I thought it happened to everyone. It was only when I started sharing my experiences that I found out they were far from normal.

My dad was the one I turned to most. Something would happen and I'd pop around or pick up the phone, 'Hey Dad, it's happened again.' At certain points in my life they were that frequent I could have entered the award for, 'Son who rang the most'.

I knew what he'd say, same thing he always said: 'You should write a book about them.' I said, 'Yeah, yeah' the way you do, thinking, parents! Me, a book? 'Have you seen how busy I am, Dad?' After a while his, 'You should write a book about them,' got shortened to, 'One for the book, son,' to be accompanied by a dad-style smile and a nod.

Well what do you know, one day I sat at the computer and began writing my story. I guess Dads really do know best. Once I started, I couldn't stop. It wasn't that it was cathartic because it wasn't. It was more… It was more a realisation that the coincidences, and I use that word because I don't know what else to call them, - although it doesn't really do them justice but it'll have to do for now, - the coincidences were speed bumps in my life. Sleeping policemen. There to wake me up, slow me down, go, 'Hey Nick this is the right road, just cool it, okay?'

It was like someone, something, some-I-don't-know was keeping me on the straight and narrow, and I began looking out for them. Anticipating them. Looking forward to them. They became talismans. Little inklings that I was going in the correct direction, and when you start from nothing,

1

and I mean nothing, and your goal is to become an honest-to-God multimillionaire, some directional assistance is a little bit welcome.

I was seventeen when I started my courier company. My very first office was also my bedroom in my dad's house, with a map of Birmingham on the wall and a telephone extension connected via a lead that ran down the stairs so you had to be careful not to trip on it when on your way up and down. Twenty-six years later I sold that company for many millions. Pretty cool when you think about it.

But the coincidences didn't stop. They've never stopped. One even happened the other day. I still look out for them, and I still love them. They're a part of me, a quirky side that make me smile and makes me feel good. This book is a way of sharing them. It's also a document on how to reach success through business - how to muscle and bustle and graft your way to early retirement. It's a travelogue, a property portfolio, and a love story. But mostly it's about the coincidences, because although they often freaked me out, they were always welcome as a sign I was doing okay, and it feels wrong to let them slip away unheard.

*Nick Terry - December 2021*

# Chapter One

I sat at the bottom of the stairs listening to my mum. She was upstairs in her bedroom, crying. My parents were arguing, Dad shouting at her, 'Tell me the truth!'

Silence, then her voice sounding strong and defiant, 'Don't you dare hit me.'

Scuffling, but it didn't sound like fighting. More like rummaging. Then his voice, loud, confident. 'Well put your hand on the Bible and swear you're not sleeping with him.'

I glanced around the hallway, between the pile of shoes kicked off inside the front door; the telephone on the table; the stack of coats piled on the banister above me, my older brother Paul's blue anorak on top; the bubbly off-white papered ceiling with the dark stain in one corner; the psychedelic orange wallpaper; the frayed carpet. I had never heard them argue before, certainly not enough to make each other cry. I was ten years old and until this point thought we were a happy family.

Dad was crying more than Mum. Unable to move, I sat listening to them for ages, my insides getting colder and emptier as the minutes ticked by until it felt as though there was this huge cavernous space opening up within me that you could have marched a battalion of soldiers through.

Had she sworn on the Bible as he'd asked? It was difficult to tell, but I guessed not. It was such a strange thing for him to have said because we were not a religious family, and I can't ever remember going to church. But I knew swearing on a Bible meant you couldn't lie.

When listing to adults sob, the sound goes up and down: loud then soft, loud then soft. During one of the soft bits, the ability to move my limbs returned and I ran fast as I could through the house and out into the back garden.

'Paul,' I shouted, much louder than I intended, 'Mum and Dad are arguing and it's bad. Really bad.' He was at the back of the garden kneeling in front of his bike, which was upside down, resting on the saddle and the handlebars. In one hand was a spanner, and spread out on the floor were more of Dad's tools.

'What do you want me to do about it?' he said, not even bothering to turn around.

'You don't understand. He asked her to swear on a Bible that she wasn't sleeping with someone. I don't think she did.'

Sighing, he said, 'Go away.'

'But…'

'GO AWAY!'

Paul was three years older than me and made it clear I was just his annoying little brother. But this wasn't little brother stuff. This was different.

I couldn't go back to sitting on the stairs, but I couldn't stand there in the garden with Paul either, so I hopped from foot to foot. Then I got it. Dashing back into the house, I yelled, 'Mum, Dad, I'm going to Richard's house,' and legged it.

Dodging the puddles in the back alley, I ran the five doors down and darted through his back gate, banging open his kitchen door without even knocking. Startled, Richard's mum spun around. She had been washing up and still had a plate in her hands, the suds now dripping on the floor. 'What on earth!' she said.

Despite the fact that Richard was a whole year younger than me – and when you're ten that's the difference between Thunderbirds and Batman, yes, THAT big a deal – he was my best friend. We used to knock about together whenever we weren't in school, and we'd often have tea in each other's houses.

One look from Richard's mum and I started bawling. You couldn't have stopped the tears with a Jubilee clip. They soaked my cheeks, and with each heave of my chest they dropped on the floor, which was taking quite the soaking between me and the dripping plate.

'Nick? Oh my gosh what's wrong?' she said, her body instantly softening as she enveloped me in a comforting hug that only made the sobbing worse. Richard must have heard, because when she finally released me and I opened my eyes he was sitting at the kitchen table watching me.

Between the gasping and the sobbing and a runny nose that she dabbed with a corner of a tissue, I told her everything.

'Oh, it will be fine,' she said a little too confidently. 'Mums and dads often have little arguments.'

She was being kind, but I knew this was no little argument. Placing me next to Richard at the table, she gave us orange juice and cake, but I didn't touch either. I expected Richard to smash into his, but copying me, he just played with his too.

We were still squidging sticky fingers into the cake when Mum burst in. I know all kids think their mums are beautiful, but mine really was. She had long thick hair that had natural body to it and she always dressed in the latest fashion.

The second she came in, any attempt she'd made to compose herself failed. Poor Richard's mum. Poor my mum.

Poor Dad.

She was crying and Richard's mum was holding her, and that vast cold empty space yawned open inside me again.

'Upstairs and play, you two,' Richard's mum said.

We didn't argue, but rather than play, we crouched at the top of the stairs and tried to listen.

'Can you hear anything?' Richard whispered.

'Shush!' But I couldn't. Turning, I sat with my back to the banister rail.

We lived in Harborne, a nice suburb of Birmingham, in a terraced house, which I guess was built in the late fifties. It was a traditional home, with a posh lounge at the front for best and Christmas, a living room in the middle, kitchen and bathroom at the back. Upstairs, you'd normally find two bedrooms. At least, that's what all the other houses in the street had, including Richard's. But Dad was clever and had worked hard over the years improving ours. Now if you went in there, you'd find the two living rooms downstairs knocked into one to create a large lounge, an extended kitchen, three bedrooms upstairs along with the bathroom, and even an en-suite shower room to the master bedroom that Mum called, 'Very ahead of its time.'

The day I moved out of the shared room with Paul and into the converted loft room I'd helped build with Dad was the best day of my life so far.

I always found it really comforting when Dad was building at home. I loved the different smells, the cutting of wood or the smell of glue, and even the smell of burning if Dad was doing some plumbing and joining copper pipes together with flux and solder. I also loved the sound of Radio One blasting away as he worked. I even loved the dust. But most of all I loved the feeling of coming in from school to see what progress he'd made. With the wooden banisters digging into my back as I sat next to Richard, and the sounds of the two women talking downstairs maddeningly too quiet to hear, I wondered if I'd ever be that happy again.

All my life Dad had worked for himself. He was a gas fitter and plumber and could turn his hand to almost any project no matter how complicated. Knock down a wall? Not a bother. Rebuild it? Simple as. Plaster? Done in a jiffy. Need your house rewired, madam? Do I know someone who could take care of it? Do I! He even repaired cars or fixed broken televisions. If it was playing up and needed someone to look at it, my dad was your man. However, on books, invoicing, accounts and records of his work, he wasn't so hot. Which is where mum came in. She was a whizz at that sort of thing, and together they made—

I closed my eyes and dug my fingernails into the palm of my hand and pushed my back into the banisters behind me as hard as I could.

—together they made the perfect team.

In addition to doing Dad's books, Mum worked part-time for Granada Rentals, where you could rent a colour television for two pounds a week, or, if that was a stretch too far, a black and white one for a quid.

'Nick. Come down here.' It was Mum's voice.

Both Richard and I bolted down the stairs, our feet touching every other step. In the kitchen both ladies were standing by the back door. Mum smiled and said, 'Time to go back, son.'

# Chapter Two

Nick Terry!'

The headmaster was standing in the doorway, sleeves rolled up and massive hairy arms crossed, his feet wide apart. At first I wasn't sure what I was supposed to do. I'd never been called out of class before. Should I gather my things and take them with me or leave them there?

He sighed as I sat there unmoving and staring at him. Then he shifted his feet closer together and dropped his arms. 'Bring everything with you, son, and hurry up.'

With the eyes of the entire class burning into me, I began packing up.

One of the other kids whispered, 'What's happening?'

I said nothing but kept on packing, shoving writing pads, books and pens into my bag.

'Maybe his mum's dead,' someone else said.

That stopped me.

'Or his house has burnt down,' another hissed.

'Or his dad's been taken to prison. That's what happened to me.'

The crazier the theories got the more relaxed I felt. I even smiled when someone said it was probably something to do with alien abductions.

The teacher said, 'That'll do. He doesn't need a commentary. Nick, you ready?'

Shoving the last thing into my bag, I stood up and nodded.

Outside, the head put his hand on my shoulder as we walked along the empty hallway. I hadn't seen or heard from Dad since the argument, though I think there had been some late-night phone calls between him and Mum.

I desperately wanted to talk to Mum about it, but I wasn't sure how to. Bumbling and muttering, I tried to one morning but she shut me down, so I did my best not to think about it, which of course meant I thought about it all the more. Was this something to do with that?

Or was it something else?

There were tales of kids taken into the head's office and caned, while others were expelled never to be seen again. If the stories in the playground were to be believed, hundreds of children had either vanished from the face of the earth or never sat down again for the rest of their lives. Was this going to happen to me? What had I done?

Then I spotted Mum and wasn't sure whether to be relieved or not.

Dad. It had to be something to do with Dad. Oh God.

It was like passing a parcel; the head's hand was still on my shoulder as he pushed me forward, and Mum put her hand on the other side to take receipt of me before he withdrew his. I almost expected someone to say, 'Do you want me to sign for him?'

Walking towards the car, a red Mini, in which I could see Paul sitting in the front passenger seat having already bagged the number one position, I said, 'What's up, Mum?'

From the age of five I'd been making my own way to and from Harborne Primary School in Station Road, sometimes on the number 3 bus but mostly on foot with a pocket full of sweets instead of wasting money on the fare. Mum collecting me from school like this felt massive.

With a quick glance down she said, 'Me and your dad have split up.'

I waited for the rest of it, keeping step with her so I wouldn't miss a thing. But that was it. No more discussion. No explanation. Nothing. Zero, zilch, nada, that's all she said.

Questions bottlenecked in my throat and had a punch-up for control of my tongue. Why? Where is Dad now? Is it my fault? Will I still see him? Does he still love me? Why don't you love him? And the biggie, did you swear on the Bible like he asked?

'We're going to live in a new house, start a new life, a new beginning,' she said, then, widening her shoulders and lifting her head, added, 'With my new boyfriend.'

Well that at least answered one question.

I felt sick as we reached the car, and she opened the driver's side door and pulled up her seat so I could climb into the rear. I even looked back at the school wishing I was still inside, sitting in class, doing maths. Anything but this.

Paul didn't look at me as I sat down in the back. She must have collected him first. Was he as shocked at this as me? It was difficult to tell.

Mum started the car and turned the radio up, killing any chance of follow-up questions, and drove and drove and drove. She drove for what felt like hours, first through the busy city traffic, then faster along country lanes. The lanes were windy and twisty, and I'd started a game in my head to look at the village signs and remember them as we passed through, fixing the route in my head.

The final village, when Mum turned down the radio and said, 'We're here,' was Hawling. We'd passed the Cotswolds road sign some time back, and it just felt like the middle of nowhere. Sure the houses were pretty if you like that sort of thing, but I yearned for our house, on our road with my bedroom, and Richard five doors up.

She pulled up outside a tiny end-of-terrace house clad in Cotswold stone called Yew Tree Cottage. She turned the engine off, and the silence imploded and took most of the air with it, making it hard to breathe.

None of us moved. Mum was staring at the front door, so I did too. Were we waiting for a sign, some sort of signal to proceed?

Then she wilted, her body softening as though she'd reached a decision. Sometimes I wonder what it was. For many years, the resentment, bordering on hatred, that I had for what she did that day to Dad and me and our family was a boulder I carried inside me every day. But looking back now I can see it couldn't have been easy for her either. However, that doesn't mean that in dreams I don't reimagine that moment in the car outside Yew Tree Cottage with Paul sitting next to Mum up front, all of us staring at the front door, Mum making up her mind to go ahead with our new life, and in the reimagining, rather than sitting there scared and confused and vulnerable, I reach over and touch her on the shoulder where her pink minidress met her shiny brown hair, and talk to her, discuss what she was doing like two adults. Weigh up if it was what she really wanted. To break apart our family. To destroy my dad. And for what? For whom?

Then we'd turn the car around and zip back through all the villages I'd remembered and she'd run crying into my dad's arms.

But of course none of that actually happened.

What really happened was the front door to the cottage opened. As it did, Mum said, 'You know him. My boyfriend. At least you already know him.'

As the man stepped into view I blinked, one of those big slow-motion blinks you do when you're not sure whether to believe your eyes.

Oh yes, I knew him all right.

# Chapter Three

I couldn't understand it. No matter how I tried to frame it in my mind it wouldn't fit. Mum and… Mr Knight. Her boss from Granada Rentals. Her boss. Mr Knight. And Mum. He was the one she left Dad for? He was the one she wouldn't swear on the Bible she hadn't slept with? Mr Knight. Are you kidding me? At least I thought if she was leaving Dad for someone else it would be a step up, like Paul Newman or one of the Beatles. But… Mr Knight. Seriously?

If ever a man was born to wear beige corduroy trousers and tank-top pullovers, it was Mr Knight. And that pretty much tells you everything you need to know about him.

He was standing in the open doorway to the cottage looking oddly grumpy for someone who had just eloped with his lover.

'Come on,' Mum said, opening the car door, but before she got out she swivelled towards me, adding, 'And Nick, be nice, okay?'

'Me? What about Paul, doesn't he have to be nice too?'

'You know what I mean,' she said, but I truly didn't.

Of course, I was never going to like Ralph Knight. After all, he had broken up our happy family and torn apart my childhood, although as it turned out I didn't need to go in with a preconceived dislike towards the situation because Ralph took care of that matter all by himself without the need for any intervention by me.

He greeted Mum on the doorstep with a hug but not a kiss, and to me he gave a look that was impossible to misunderstand, his arm wrapped proprietorially around my mum. The look he gave said: you're here under sufferance because there's nowhere else for you to go. Be good and behave yourself… or else.

It was so nice to be wanted! And singled out; it was like Paul didn't exist! Where was his look of 'Your card is marked, Sunny Jim.' Why was it all pointed at me?

Inside, the cottage was dark and smelled of cold and damp. Apparently the owners were friends of 'Ralph. Call me Ralph.' Oh gee, and I thought I was going to get to call you Dad. It was a holiday home, and the owners said the happy couple could use it as a bolthole for a few weeks until they got something more permanent sorted.

After a quick scout around I deduced there were only two bedrooms, which meant I was back sharing with Paul. Great. However, there was one genuine upside to this cottage, though it had nothing to do with the cottage itself but rather what was twenty foot away outside. A red telephone box.

It was a couple of days until I managed to get a moment alone with Mum where 'Oh Ralph, you're so good with the boys' wasn't around. What did she see in him? It's not rhetorical, I really mean it: what did she see in him? And as for being good with us… If self-centred, meanness, grumpy and shouting when he didn't get his own way was an indication of being good with children, then 'Will you please stop calling me Mr Knight, Nick. It's Ralph, okay?' should have a career as a children's TV presenter. Crackerjack maybe.

We were in the kitchen. Ralph was probably having a lie down.

'Mum,' I said quietly, 'can I phone Dad please?' We'd both clocked the red telephone box outside.

'No.'

'But…'

'No buts. No.'

'But Mum, please.'

Stopping what she was doing, she turned to face me. For a while she didn't say anything, just stood looking at me. She was wearing another from her wardrobe of fashionable tiny minidresses, this one a dusty yellow, her hair not up in a bun but down and glamorous even though she was doing housework. I saw the way people looked at her. The double takes from men, the darker looks from women who didn't know her; and to be fair when her back was turned and only I could see from some that did, I felt proud to have such a pretty mum. It just felt like she'd thrown it all away to be cooped up in this smelly cottage, like having a beautiful bird locked in a cage and shoved under the stairs.

Then she said, 'You can't tell him where we are.'

'Okay,' I agreed, feeling my heart lurch and unsure if it was for Mum's kindness or the excitement of speaking to Dad.

'I mean it, Nick. You have to promise, promise faithfully, that you won't say where we are.'

'What if he asks me, Mum?'

She thought for a second. 'If he does, tell him the truth. Tell him that I have said you can't, and if he asks once more you won't be allowed to call again. But you have to promise, that's really important, Nick. Do you understand?'

I wanted to ask her 'Do you want me to swear on a Bible now?' but instead just said, 'Yes, Mum.'

Desperate to hear Dad's voice, there was one last thing I had to do. Bombing up the stairs as quietly as I could – no way I wanted to wake Ralph – I found Paul lying on his bed reading a football comic.

Brandishing three two-pence coins Mum had given me, I said, 'Paul, Mum said we can phone Dad. Come on.'

I expected him to jump up, but he just turned over. I asked a couple more times but it was clear he was ignoring me. Fine, suit yourself.

Not wanting to waste a second more, I made my way outside, cutting across the grass. The door to the phone box was really heavy and hard to open. I had to put all my effort into pulling it back wide enough to nip inside. As soon as the door closed behind me I realised I'd been holding my breath, and little by little I let it out, expecting the new breath in to have that familiar scent of urine – well I did grow up in Birmingham. But it wasn't there. It must be all the bushes in the countryside, I decided. Pissed men have somewhere to go other than phone boxes. Swiftly I dialled the number.

Dad answered on the third ring. I rammed a two-pence piece into the slot and for the first minute he told me over and over how pleased he was to hear from me and how much he missed me. Then the sound of pips cut in over what he was saying to me so I rammed the second two-pence piece into the slot. The next minute was a little trickier, as we tackled the awkward topic of why Paul wasn't with me. More pips and my last coin.

The third minute he started crying. 'I love you, Dad. I'll call you every week, I promise.' I was doing a lot of promising today.

'I love you too, son,' he sobbed back. Then the pips again: the money had run out, time was up and we were cut off. The silence was deafening.

As I replaced the receiver, I thought, at least he didn't ask where we were.

The promise I made to call him every week was one I kept for the next three or four weeks, but the calls got harder to make as he would always end up crying, so in the end I just stopped calling.

After eight weeks Mum and 'Do they really have to eat that much? They're small boys and food's very expensive you know' found a place to rent in a nearby village called Stanton. That was when I started back at school, which was only a couple of miles away in the village of Laverton. It was a very small school and completely different from the junior school I had attended in Harborne. Laverton junior school only had a total of twenty-five kids, ranging from five to eleven years old. Being ten myself made me the oldest bar one. There were only two teachers: the head, who lived on the premises, called Miss Mills, and her assistant Miss Brown.

Six months later, we moved again, to another village called Notgrove. Despite my parents' situation, some of my happiest memories are living and growing up in Notgrove. When we first moved to this village there were still a few weeks to go before the summer half-term break. When the holiday was over I would be moving up from a junior school to a senior school located in Bourton-on-the-Water called Bourton Vale, which was a comprehensive – yes, despite Miss Mills best efforts I failed my eleven-plus!

Mum thought it was too late in the school year to find me a new junior school, so for the next few weeks Mum and I would get up early and she would drive me from Notgrove to Laverton, a distance of about fifteen miles.

Reaching home one day, my bag next to me containing some particularly fiendish chemistry homework that I'd already decided not to bother tackling, I had a sudden feeling of 'Dad'. No, feeling's not the right word. It was more like a vision, as though I could see him there, right there. I could sense him, I could smell him, I could feel him; not emotionally, it was as though I could reach out and physically touch him.

It was raining as we pulled up on the driveway. 'Dad's been here,' I shouted.

Feeling panicked, Mum was whipping her head back and forth. 'What do you mean he's here? Where?' She sounded terrified.

'No. He's not here now. But he's been here today. I just know it.'

Her face crinkled in a mix of confusion and anger. 'Get out,' she said.

We both opened our doors just as a neighbour came rushing over to us. 'Oh Alison, can I have a quick word please?' she said with a slight panic in her tone.

Startled, and clearly a little creeped out by all this, she said, 'Okay. Sure. I'll just let Nick in the house and I'll come round.'

'Er, no. Straight away would be good.'

# Chapter Four

Dad had been at the house. The police had even been called when one of the neighbours spotted him smashing a window in the back door. The presumption was he was trying to get in, although why he would do that was more of a mystery. When the cops arrived, he scarpered. Well you would, wouldn't you.

I have no idea how I knew he'd been there. It's not like we'd even spoken recently. Mum grilled me relentlessly, and to this day I'm bemused. But what I do know is that was the start. That right there was the moment it all began: the coincidences, the knowing things I couldn't possibly know, the feeling that this world is far smaller than you might think.

My life, my business success, is in part down to these events, almost as though there was some intervening hand jutting down from on high and moving the figures around this giant chessboard that is my life, so the right people are shifted into the right positions at precisely the right time for me to take advantage.

I can't describe it in any other way, although there was this really interesting study carried out where a bunch of actors were seated individually at tables in a café, with one super successful businessperson hidden amongst them. A cross section of unsuspecting members of the public were then told to go in, get a drink and find someone to sit next to. When later quizzed, the people who sat next to the businessperson and struck up a conversation described themselves as generally lucky in life. Whereas those who plonked themselves down with an actor, sipped their drink quietly and left, felt they were generally unlucky. Put me in that café and I guarantee I'd end up beside that businessperson, chatting away like

I've got all my words to use up that day. Does that make me lucky? Maybe. But there's more to it than that. A heck of a lot more.

'You must know,' Mum insisted. We were sitting at the kitchen table, Ralph fixing the broken window pane behind us. 'Had Dad said something to you?'

'I haven't spoken to him, Mum. I promise. I just knew. That's all.'

Clearly she didn't believe me, but with nothing else to go on she wrapped up the inquisition, for now anyway, and I was allowed to go off and play. I didn't go far. I could still hear them talking in hushed whispers.

'Of course the boy knows more than he's saying, my love,' Ralph said. 'All I'm saying is, we're going to have to be careful what we tell him from now on. We can't trust him.'

'He's my son!' Mum whispered loudly. 'I will not treat him like that. If he says he doesn't know how he knew, then I believe him.'

'But do you? Think about what you're saying. He must have been talking to him and now he's too scared to admit it. It's the only thing that makes any sense.'

Silence. The noise of a kettle being put on, tools being put away. Then I went to my room and stayed there for the rest of the night.

Slowly, routine returned. Mum took me to school, picked me up again and brought me home. I did homework, had tea, and went out to play. The village was amazing and I loved it there. It was wholly owned by the Aclands, who lived in the manor house next to a beautiful Anglican church, within which I found ancient effigies and tombs of the Whittington family, descendants of Dick Whittington. I sat for hours in there wondering what it must have been like for Dick, who couldn't have been much older than me, to leave home with empty pockets in search of his fortune. How must that have felt? Was he scared? Was he excited?

Having recently sat my eleven-plus, the exam that denotes whether you go to a grammar or comprehensive school, and failed, I knew I wasn't academic. I didn't need a report card, teachers or my mother to tell me that. But that didn't feel so important. I knew I was going to be a success. I just knew it. Like Dick, if I had to walk from here to London to make something of myself, I would. I'd do it in scruffy old boots with empty pockets just like him. I'd sleep on the sides of roads in ditches too if I had to.

Truth is, I was going to be a millionaire. If anyone asked me what I was going to be when I grew up, that's what I told them. 'I'm going to be a millionaire,' I'd say. Mum always told me to be honest and tell the truth, so I did. It felt as natural and real as saying I wanted to be a train driver, or a policeman. If Dick Whittington could do it, then why not Nick Terry?

'Nick, we're going to be late for school,' Mum shouted up the stairs. It had been about three weeks since the Dad break-in incident, and while nothing tangible had changed, there was a sense of holding back around me. When I walked into rooms, Mum and Ralph would go quiet or there'd be an obvious change of subject. Things were talked about in vague platitudes, such as where Mum would be that day: 'Oh you know, out and about.' It made me feel lonely and isolated, as though I was disappearing into myself somehow, talking less and less at home. I even felt I must be a distrustful person, bad somehow, though goodness knows why, I hadn't done anything wrong. But I felt as though I had, which is almost as bad.

'Coming,' I called back, gathering my things and nipping down the stairs.

With the eleven-plus exam now behind me, and my fate, certainly as far as my future education was concerned, decided, I still had a couple of weeks left at my old school in Laverton.

We clambered into the car and Mum would always put on Radio Two as we bombed along the country lanes trying to catch up time.

The habit I developed when we first left Dad for Yew Tree Cottage of memorising routes had morphed into road names. Just out of Lower Coscombe is Stanway Hill, a long, winding, very steep hill. Just as the car approached the first right-hand bend Mum suddenly screamed, 'I've got no brakes!'

Shooting her a look, I could see the colour had drained from her face. I guess it had from mine too. She had both hands on the steering wheel, gripping it for all she was worth, while her foot pumped the pedal. We weren't slowing one iota.

This was bad, bad, bad. Stanway Hill isn't an average hill. The incline, the twists, the main road crossing it at the bottom all meant we didn't stand a chance.

She continued pumping the pedal for all she was worth but the car wasn't slowing. I could hear her breathing above the radio, could see her hands turning white on the steering wheel as she gripped harder and harder.

We took the first bend way faster than was safe, the tyres making screeching noises as they fought to keep in contact with the tarmac. All too quickly we were flung out of that bend and onto the main straight like a racing car on a quick lap.

'Mum?' I said, loading the word with all the questions I wanted answering but knowing none would be forthcoming. She didn't even look across at me. She didn't have time.

'Jesus!' she screamed.

# Chapter Five

I've never understood the 'if I can't have you, nobody can' mindset. Don't get me wrong, I've had my heart broken and wished with all my being that she ends up alone and drunk cleaning out a cat litter tray at two in the morning. But it never lasted, and I certainly didn't fantasise about killing anyone. That's insanity. Literally.

Hurtling down Stanway Hill, the brakes gone, Mum dipped the clutch and forced the gear lever down into third, the old Mini shuddering and jerking as the engine bit, forcing me up and into my seatbelt with the momentum of the sudden downshift. By going down the gears and applying the handbrake, we slowed just enough to steer into a small lay-by where Mum aimed for a tree stump, the car crunching into it and bringing us to a complete stop.

She turned off the engine, both of us staring ahead. Breathing hard she said, 'Are you okay?'

I mumbled I was.

'Good.'

'What happened?'

'I … don't know. Dear God,' she said, sweeping her hair back with one hand.

A car pulled up behind. Mum looked in the mirror and said, 'Isn't that…?'

For the first time ever I hoped when I spun around I wouldn't see my dad. Grabbing the back of Mum's seat for purchase, I forced myself to look. It wasn't Dad. At first I didn't recognise who it was, not because I didn't know her, but because of that odd disconnect when you spot someone out of the environment in which you're so used to seeing them. It was only when she got out of her car it twigged. It was my teacher, Miss Brown. Hers was the very next car to come along.

There is a theory that's both utterly nuts and completely plausible that there's only five hundred real people in the world, which is why if you decide to sunbathe naked on a secluded Spanish beach it's a fait accompli your old primary school teacher will wander by. Or if you have a crash down a very steep hill in the Cotswolds!

Making her way to Mum's side of the car, Miss Brown exclaimed, 'Goodness, are you both okay?' Judging by her face she was as surprised to see us as we her. 'Nick? Is that you?' she said, peering across at me.

'Good morning, Miss Brown,' I said brightly, and smiled the way only a kid can after a near-death experience, just stopping myself from adding, 'And how are you today?'

'Honestly, we're fine,' said Mum.

'Are you sure?' replied Miss Brown.

'Absolutely,' confirmed Mum.

Miss Brown offered, 'Would you like me to take Nick in to school?'

'Oh, would you?' Mum said, a little too enthusiastically for my liking. 'That would be fantastic.'

Actually we both went, Mum zipping into the head's office as soon as we got there to use the phone and me hoping that at least a few of the other kids spotted her, as I knew from experience having a pretty mother would increase my standing in the playground hierarchy no end.

It was two days until we got the phone call from the garage. I wasn't supposed to know, but I overheard. The brake pipe had been cut deliberately. By the time we reached the top of Stanway Hill all the fluid had drained out. We were lucky. Very lucky.

As for the culprit, there was only one candidate. Oh Dad, what were you thinking?

It was years until I could talk to him about it. After all, his actions could have killed us. Killed Mum. Killed me. How do you bring that up? 'Hey Dad, remember that time you tried to kill Mum and me?'

Actually, that's pretty much how it happened.

I was eighteen. I'd lived with the knowledge of what he'd done for all those years. Dad and I were close. He was by far my biggest supporter, my mentor, my best friend. But I felt like it was there in the room with us every time we were together. A shadow just at the edge of vision. A shadow with a silent voice: 'He could have killed you and your mother. Your dad, his actions, could have killed you.'

Fear kept me quiet for all those years. Fear of what he'd say if I pulled him on it. Fear of how I'd react; how I'd have to react. But then in the end it was fear that drove to me bring it up. Fear that if it wasn't aired, if it was kept secret, it would inevitably drive us apart. And that fear was much bigger.

So I did. It wasn't planned, wasn't thought through, I just said, 'Dad, remember that time you tried to kill Mum and me?'

I'd had a job close by and dropped in on my way back to the office. He was sitting on the sofa, his work day finished, smiling, unaware of the conversation we were about to have. To be fair so was I, yet as soon as I started I knew with every fibre in my body that this was the right thing to do.

His smile dropped, along with his gaze, which settled on the floor between his feet.

'You cut the brake pipe on the car. I overheard Mum talking to the mechanic. Did you know the route we'd take? Did you know we'd go down Stanway Hill? It's okay, I just... Why? Why did you do it?'

Silence, but not silence. Two people who are close communicate all the time. Lovers, family, best friends, even enemies continually swap signals on how they're feeling and what they're thinking. Dad seemed to shrink, to get physically smaller. His breathing shallowed. His eyes shut. The silence of him not speaking was deafening. Then he broke it by saying, 'I didn't know you knew.'

More loud silence. Movement in his seat, as though he were uncomfortable but didn't want to shift too much. A stroke of his head, his hands still grubby from a day of plumbing, even though he'd scrubbed them when he got in.

'I...' he began. 'I didn't mean it. When I realised what I'd done, I... Oh God. Nick,' his eyes opened again but his attention was fixed on the floor. 'I thought she'd phone me. I thought she'd see the puddle of oil under the car and phone me like she always did. If there was a problem, I'd fix it. That's what I did. She should have called me, then I'd go round and mend it. I just wanted to see her. Nick, I just wanted to see her. I couldn't bear that she'd left me. I wanted her back, of course I did. I wanted her to need me, to realise that I was there for her. To do things. Make life easier, better... I don't know. But, failing that, I just wanted to see her.' Now he looked up, and I could see the tears running down his face.

'I loved her. She was everything. I missed her. My heart, it… I couldn't think. I couldn't function. She left me. I just wanted to see her. I didn't know what I was doing. I just remember trying to get her to need me, and she always called me if there was a problem with the car. I thought she'd see the spilled oil and call me.'

There was so much hurt in his face, I did something the dynamic of our father-son relationship had never called for before. Reaching across, I gently placed my hand on top of his, which may not sound much, but it felt like such a grown-up thing to do, especially to your dad, and only proved to make his tears fall even faster.

'I was out of my mind. But I didn't try and kill you or your mother. I just tried to make her need me. I'm so sorry.'

And that was it. The first and last time we spoke about it.

Craziness apart, I loved living at Notgrove, which was basically a huge farm estate. Apart from a couple of grander houses that were privately owned, and one or two cottages that were rented, ours being number seven, everyone else in the village worked for the estate, including a gardener, a gamekeeper, stable-hand, dairyman, a carpenter, dry stone wall specialist and numerous farm labourers. Living next door to me was Robert Brain and his family. Bob, as he liked to be called, was the shepherd.

Built like a boxer, Bob was friendly and had a lot of time for the kids in the village, including three of his own. Whenever I could I would go to work with him, sitting on the back of the trailer that he pulled with his little Massey Ferguson 125 tractor as we headed down the road towards the fields. Sitting next to me would be one of his three sheepdogs.

Lambing season was my favourite time of year, even though it meant having to get up at five in the morning most weekends. Dark and bitterly cold, I loved it. I'm convinced my work ethic of putting in long hours stemmed from this time, as did my love of animals.

Once we had arrived in the fields Bob would allow me to drive the tractor, a real treat for an eleven-year-old. A few years later I passed my driving test after just one lesson, a week after my seventeenth birthday. I didn't tell the examiner most of my driving experience had been in fields.

Then, out of the blue after four glorious years living at Notgrove, Mum announced we were moving to Amersham in Buckinghamshire because of Ralph's job.

That night I lay awake in bed staring at the wall. The rest of the house was silent except for the occasional cry of my new half-brother, Peter, and the sounds that accompanied it of Mum or Ralph getting up to give him a bottle.

We'd all got used to having a baby in the house. What I wouldn't ever get used to is leaving here. Why did we have to go? Couldn't Ralph get a job locally?

'No. I'm not going,' I'd said when they'd told me earlier that day, sitting at the kitchen table with Mum and Ralph both busying themselves making tea for us and the baby.

'Don't be so silly, Nick, of course you're going,' she said.

'Why? You can't make me.'

'Actually we can,' said Ralph. 'And we will.'

'But I don't want to!' I screamed, slamming my chair back and hurling myself out of the room.

So there I was, in bed staring at the wall in the pitch dark of night contemplating not only the end of my time there, but a new beginning someplace else. My body felt heavy, like I was squashing myself into the mattress to the point where I couldn't move, couldn't even roll over. The only part that wasn't heavy were my eyelids. They were as light as one of Bob's new-born lambs.

Life was unfair, and there was nothing I could do about it. Yet I knew it was more than that, although that in itself was enough to make me scream into the pillow and punch the living daylights out of the bed. But I knew that was just the knee-jerk. The frustration of being pulled away from a way of life I'd fallen in love with without any consideration to me. Call it teenage angst, or selfishness, or whatever, and I could feel that anger throughout my stuck-to-the-bed body; it felt warm and alive and impossible to ignore. However, that was not a tenth of it.

I was fifteen. My voice had broken. My body was changing, and most of the changes were deeply embarrassing and confusing. Every feeling inside me felt overwhelming, and I couldn't work out how to control them. Like the hurling myself out of the kitchen earlier when Mum told me we were moving. Throwing that kind of tantrum wasn't me, but I wasn't in charge. Something else was. Something that scared me, not because it was violent, but because it was unknown. What I hated was that there was nobody I could speak to about it all. Ralph didn't get on with me, would seldom even acknowledge I existed unless it was to yell at me, and since the baby had arrived Mum had no time for me either. As for Paul, forget it. I felt so alone, and so confused. I missed my dad. I missed the way of life I believed we would have had if Mum hadn't shacked up with Mr Bloody Ralph Knight. I desperately wanted my dad to be proud of me. He was the only person who understood. Now he never would, not if they took away from me the only things in my crappy life I could rely on and understand: the estate, the people who worked here, my very best friend Gordon Creed and the farm animals. Leaving me with nothing. Nothing at all. Tears tickled my cheeks and I couldn't even summon the energy to wipe them away.

Driving out of the village for the last time remains one of the unhappiest days of my life. In our car was Mum, Ralph, baby Peter and the dog Fred. As we followed our removal van out and away, I sat on the back seat sobbing quietly. Arrangements had been made for Paul to live with a school friend in Winchcombe so he could finish his final exams at Cheltenham Grammar School. I would not see Paul again for many years after that.

The journey took forever, but eventually we arrived in Amersham and parked up outside our newly rented semi-detached council house. It had a small front garden and an even smaller back garden. You couldn't get further away from a working country estate if you tried. I was allocated a bedroom, which was damp and dark. Mum and Ralph had the biggest bedroom with just enough space for their double bed and Peter's cot. But that wasn't the worst thing about the move. That juicy little nugget was reserved for Amersham Boys Comprehensive. My new school.

The hierarchy of the form room I'd been given was long established, with most of the boys coming through the system together from year one. They knew each other's quirks, weaknesses, and, in the case of the bullies, strengths. You could taste the aggression in the air. When I arrived – new uniform, odd accent, a combination of Gloucestershire and Brummie – I stood out, and all that aggression in the class got a focus.

It was hell, and I loathed it. So I made a decision. A logical, considered, informed decision. I had to escape. I had to run away.

# Chapter Six

So,' the man said, taking his glasses off with one hand and pinching the bridge of his nose with the other, 'tell me what you want to do with your life after school.'

We were in an empty classroom sitting opposite one another at the top table, desks in neat lines behind us. To the left a window ran the entire length of one wall, which would afford you, if you took the trouble to use it, the view of another brick wall some ten feet away. Mind you, some said if you ducked down low enough and peered up, you could spot sky. I'll have to take their word for it.

Even during lesson times, a school is never quiet. There's a hum, not unlike that of a beehive; a sort of busy background noise that blends in so after a while you don't even notice it. Unless you're new. Hum, hum, hum, hum, hum, it went. Hum, hum, hum, hum.

Papers shuffled. 'Um, Nick, isn't it?'

I nodded. Above his head on the chalkboard two words had been written: Career's Advice.

'So? What do you want to be when you leave school?'

Maybe it was the way he phrased the question – what do you want to be, rather than what do you want to do – that made me answer honestly. That or the fact that I knew full well I was running away soon, and therefore I didn't care. Either way, I looked him in the eye and said, 'I'm going to be a millionaire.'

Slamming a fist down on the paper in front of him – a fist! – he exclaimed, 'Don't be so bloody pathetic, boy! Idiot. I'm asking what you want to do with your life. This is not a joke. One day you're going to walk out of this school—'

Sooner than you think.

'—and have to face the real world. In that world you're going to need money to survive. To get money you're going to need a job. Is this sinking in, because you don't look to me as though you've got many options, and trust me, of all the options you do have, a millionaire isn't one of them. It's not even a job, it's a pipe dream. It's…' – he searched for a word, and settled on – 'stupid.'

I couldn't understand it, why was he so angry? Should I have said, oh I want to be a policeman, or drive a fire engine? Ooh ooh, I know, please can I be a footballer? No, I'm going to be a millionaire. You asked me the question and I gave you the answer. I'm going to be Dick Whittington; I'm going to walk a thousand miles and sleep in ditches and I'm going to graft and graft and graft and I am going to be successful, because what I'm not going to be is like Mum and Ralph, living at the whim of this landlord, or that employer, without a say in matters; a pawn to be shoved and pushed around. No way. Money gives you control over your own life. It allows you to be free. So I'm going to be a millionaire. I'm going to work every second of every day and then I'm going to retire at forty.

I thought of my dad, the only other person in the world I'd told of my dream. He didn't smash his fist down when I said it. Even though it was over the phone I could hear him smile. He said, 'Go for it, son.'

I haven't seen him in almost four years, not since around the time he cut the brake pipe on Mum's car. After that we all kind of decided it wouldn't be in anyone's interest to have him pop by for a friendly coffee.

Slowly I became aware of the silence in the classroom, the man on the opposite side of the desk staring at me. I looked up and caught his eye, in response to which he shook his head as though deeply saddened. It made me laugh, even though I knew that was the very worst thing I could do, but I couldn't help it.

'Shop work,' he said, and sighed, scribbling on the form in front of him. 'If you're lucky.'

Getting up, I made my way out. It was Thursday afternoon. The rest of my year were playing cricket in one of the neighbouring fields, no doubt a testosterone-filled game where at some point the bat would be used as a weapon to clunk some poor chap on the noggin. I could go and join them, but then the poor chap would most likely be me. Or I could walk out, find a phone box and kick-start my escape plan.

If anything, speaking to the career's advisor had redoubled my resolve. I hated my life. I had no friends, I loathed school, I didn't fit in at home and they didn't want me there anyway, not with the baby to worry about. Even my body was against me. I was a brain that didn't belong to anyone or anything and had nothing. Life was shit. But I did have a plan.

Walking down the corridor, the hum of work coming from the classrooms either side of me, I thrust a hand into my pocket and reached for some coins, twisting and flipping them between my fingers. The fear had been that one of the Neanderthals in my class would take them from me at lunchtime, but the call to see the career's advisor had saved me from that at least – and they say careers advice in school is worthless.

Slipping out the main entrance, I hurried along the road in the direction of the phone box. Unlike the one outside Yew Tree Cottage, this one did smell of urine. Trying not to breathe in too deeply, I dialled the familiar number. At the other end, the phone was picked up on the second ring.

'Dad?' I said breathlessly.

'Nick? Is that really you? Is everything okay?'

Despite not having seen him in person for all those years, we had kept in regular telephone contact. I'd even told him how much I hated Amersham.

Taking a deep breath I said, 'Dad, can I come and live with you?'

No silence, no beat, no pause. Not a second's consideration. 'Yes,' he said, laughing. 'Yes.' Then all the adult stuff hit. 'Are you sure? It's early days there. In a while you'll make friends and everything will look different.'

I was already shaking my head. 'I want to come and live with you in Birmingham. Please, Dad.'

He was back laughing again. 'Okay,' he said, sounding relieved and happy. 'Let's do it. Let's do it straight away, but only if you're absolutely sur—'

I cut him off with a 'Dad!'

'Okay. What time do you finish school? Three thirty, right? Your mum's not going to like it.'

'She won't even notice. She's got too much going on with Peter. I think they'll be pleased not to have me around.'

Make that I know they'll be pleased not to have me around.

'Right. Right. I'll be there tomorrow, at the school gates, three thirty.'

We said goodbye and I replaced the receiver. For the first time in forever, I felt euphoric, as though all the weight had been lifted from me. Laughing, I shouldered the door and stepped out of the phone box, breathing in the fresh carbon-dioxide air of the main road and thinking how much nicer it was than the urine stench inside.

That night I kept to myself in my room. No one questioned it. No one cared. In the morning I got up extra early and crept about packing a few essentials before quietly slipping downstairs. The house was silent around me, the only noise my own breath.

Within four weeks of leaving Notgrove, which was the worst moment of my shitty life so far, I was about to add another worst to the list. Making my way into the kitchen, I dumped my bag down and sat on the cold tiled floor, Fred wagging his tail and licking my hands.

Without Fred, I would not be alive. He was everything to me, and me to him. We were both outcasts who didn't fit in this new life Mum and Ralph were making for themselves. We didn't understand it, and we weren't part of it. We were inconveniences.

'I've got to go,' I said, unable to look him in the eye. Fred, a black Collie, rolled over onto his back with his tail swishing back and forth across the floor, his chops falling down to reveal grinning teeth. I'm not sure he knew something was up… well, until the tears started running down my cheeks, then he sat up, staring at me. He knew, he knew all right.

Explaining what I was about to do, and why, I told him everything. I told him how much I loved him, and how much I hated Mum and Ralph for what they were doing to me. With tears now streaming uncontrollably down my face, I hugged him over and over again, said I was sorry, oh so very sorry, and left the house for the final time. Goodbye, Fred.

At school I placed my bag in the locker and spent the rest of the day wishing time would go faster. It's funny how time drags when you want it to go quickly. At last, the bell rang for the end of day. Heading out the school gates I could see Dad just the other side standing by his old white clapped-out Morris Minor van. He had a massive smile on his face, and when I reached him he gave me a huge hug, then quickly told me to get into the van.

Despite everything, he had wanted to do the right thing, so he'd arrived at the school thirty minutes earlier and had spoken to the headmaster. He explained he was taking me out of school and back to Birmingham. The head had told Dad that he was legally obliged to phone Mum and explain what was going on. To this day we suspect he felt a little sorry for my dad and never made that call to Mum until well after the last bell had rung. That had given us enough time to hit the road and get a few miles away. We decided it might be prudent to drive back via B roads and not use the main A roads or motorways. As it turns out, Dad was right to be cautious.

After an hour on the road, he thought it best we pull over at the next phone box so I could call Mum and explain.

The phone rang once and was answered by a man I didn't recognise. He said he was a police officer. I asked to speak to Mum but he said no. Then he asked to speak to Dad. I handed him the receiver, feeling scared that things had escalated to the point where the police were sitting in our house waiting for the phone to ring.

After a few moments Dad put down the phone. All the colour had drained from his face. 'They want me to take you back,' he said. 'And they want me to do it right now.'

# Chapter Seven

Of course, we weren't going back. Life would be so much worse if we did. No, this was a one-way, one-chance shot.

'I think you should get in the back,' Dad said, pulling out into the line of traffic. 'The police are looking for two people in a van. If they only see one, then maybe they won't twig it's us.'

Good point. I clambered over the back of the seat to where Dad kept his tools, and found a wooden box to sit on, one he'd made himself. The smell of plumbing and oil and dust was stronger back here. It made me feel safe somehow.

Running away is exhausting. Oh sure there's the initial euphoria, that surge of adrenaline, but after a while it's just driving. Outside it was drizzling, the windscreen wipers squeaking as they intermittently scraped the drops away so Dad could see as he pushed the Morris Minor way beyond the speed it was comfortable doing, which was anything above forty.

Unlike Mum, who turned into a chimney as soon as she got with Ralph, Dad didn't smoke. 'Have you ever smoked, Dad?' I asked as it stopped drizzling outside and started raining properly. The scream of the van, the noise of the road and now the swatch-swatch, swatch-swatch of the wipers meant it was difficult to hear anything else, and for a while I wondered if he'd heard me. But he had.

'Why'd you ask?' His words were defensive, but the tone was more amused.

Shrugging, I looked out the window. It was 1975, the Vietnam War had just ended, and Margaret Thatcher was clearly manoeuvring herself to soon become Britain's first woman Prime Minister. The song that was taking the country by storm was the new one by Queen, 'Bohemian Rhapsody'. When it came on the radio I asked Dad to turn it up. He laughed and he did, and we listened to it together. When it finished he said, 'You haven't started smoking, have you, son?'

Shaking my head, I said 'no'. And I hadn't. I wanted to be like him, not like Mum and Ralph. He knew Mum was smoking now, of course, but he didn't know about the drinking, the late-night takeaways, the foreign holidays and the partying.

Blowing out his cheeks he said, 'It's hard to fathom how much she's changed. She was never into any of that when we were together. Not that I knew about, anyway.'

They'd met when they were both eighteen years old. Dad was an apprentice for British Gas and was on his first live call with his trainer at an address to fit a gas cooker. The house they arrived at was in Bournville, the home of Cadbury chocolate. Mum, who came from a very big family of seven boys and two girls, had been farmed out because her parents couldn't cope with them all, and she was living there with her auntie. She was bright, went to the local grammar school, and was quite naïve, which must have been incredibly attractive. Dad was besotted, and that feeling never changed. Bless him.

We arrived back in Birmingham late that night at a place called Yardley, a little suburb about four miles from the city centre. Dad had already thought ahead and made arrangements to stay the night with friends, Peter and Joan. Going back to his house was out of the question. In fact, he knew he couldn't go back for some time, or at least until things had settled down and Mum had accepted the idea that I was not coming home again.

The plan the following morning was to move onto a narrowboat owned by a friend of Peter and Joan's. He had agreed that Dad and I could go and live on his boat for a few days, but evidently the keys to the boat were at his weekend house. The boat itself was moored in Fradley, just outside Lichfield. The aim was to have breakfast and then make our way over to their friend's house, collect the keys and then head for Fradley.

Over a piece of toast, Dad said, 'I'm going to move the van. It's too visible where it is. I want to put it in a back street.'

As he got up, I did too. We'd move it together, the two amigos. Outside, the rain of last night had stopped and we walked in friendly silence, our footsteps in sync.

Getting in the van, I breathed the comforting smell of plumber's tools. It did it to me every time. The van was old and a bit beaten up. It didn't start first time. It didn't start second time. But third time lucky. Dad drove it a short distance and parked up in a side street, the name of which wasn't lost on me. It was Yew Tree Avenue.

I hadn't thought about Yew Tree Cottage, the place we fled to when Mum first left Dad, for a long time. It made me think of Paul, and I wondered how he was doing. It also made me think of Mum, but, like, an earlier version of her before all the drinking and the smoking and the partying. A version of her that was young and innocent and beautiful.

Back in the house, breakfast finished and cleared away, we got ready to leave. Putting our bags in the boot, Dad and I climbed onto the back seat while Peter and Joan got in the front, Peter driving. The car was a maroon Austin Allegro, and together we set off to collect the keys for the boat.

The traffic was light and so was the conversation. I liked listening to the three of them chat, liked it when they laughed. Liked it when they teased one another. I didn't speak much because I didn't want to change the mood, and felt I didn't know them enough, or trust myself enough to join in. So I alternated between looking out the window and snatching glances at Dad.

Then everything changed.

The mood, the energy in the car, the traffic, even the weather became charged. Everything felt oppressive and heavy, the way it does when there's a storm imminent. I was looking out the window, doing my thing of remembering routes and street names. Suddenly I knew where I was. I knew where I was very well. And it felt bad.

My breath felt spiky in my throat, and despite the radio and the chat going on around me, I could hear the rasp it was beginning to make out loud. I wanted to get out and run, wanted to fling open the car door and bolt. I didn't care about the traffic or the speed we were travelling. I'd take my chance. But I couldn't move. My legs felt weak and wobbly. My arms had no more strength than spaghetti.

With every turn we were getting closer.

I started crying. I couldn't stop it happening.

Glancing over at me, Dad spotted my terror. His face changed, became quizzical, confused, then worried. Reaching out, he put his hand on my arm.

'What's wrong, Nick?' he said.

'You're not going to hurt me, are you, Dad?' I said, my voice so soft and childlike.

Suddenly aware there was a problem, Dad switched the radio off, conversation ceased. For a while nobody said anything. Then the car pulled in and Peter killed the engine. 'We're here,' he said.

I looked out the window, knowing already where here was.

We were parked next to a red phone box. Beyond it was Yew Tree Cottage.

'Why would I hurt you, Nick?' Dad said. 'I don't understand.'

I pointed at the cottage. 'That's where Mum brought us when we left you. That's the phone box I used to call you from.'

Her voice soft and gentle and full of concern, Joan assured me everything was okay and nobody was going to hurt me. 'That's our friend's house. That's where we're going to collect the narrowboat keys.'

I just thought I was in some sort of trouble for never telling Dad where we had run off to when Mum first left him, but this was nothing more than an amazing coincidence. A truly amazing coincidence, and I was soon to find out, it was to be the first of many in my life.

# Chapter Eight

Being parented by Dad was a lot different to being parented by Mum. Mum's approach to looking after children involved feeding, clothing in clean, ironed clothes and setting practical boundaries, whereas Dad's was more, 'You're going to have to get on with it yourself, son.' So, I did.

When he wasn't MIA bunking down in a narrowboat with his abducted son, Dad still lived in the same house in Harborne he'd had before the split, and after some frantic negotiations the UN could learn a thing or two from, Mum agreed to let me stay with Dad and we moved back in to our family home.

That first night was weird, sitting in my old bedroom in the loft after all the years away. In a way nothing had changed, but in another everything had. It felt like the setting was correct, the house and the bedroom, but the people within it had been replaced, as though watching a TV show where they swap actors playing one of the main characters, and you think, I swear blind that's not the same one as last time. Now sitting on the bed, I'd swear blind I wasn't the same person I had been. Neither was Dad. We both looked similar to the people we had been, but inside all sorts of changes had happened. Brutal changes.

They say what doesn't kill you makes you stronger, and I guess there must be some truth to that, because a couple of days later I got myself up, made breakfast, washed, ironed my school shirt that I had brought from Amersham, and packed myself off to yet another new school.

Now here's the thing, while I hated every second of my old school – the bullying, the violence and the chaos – it had made me battle ready. Walking in to the new place I didn't feel like a victim, and that must have come across, because I seemed to blend right in with no trouble at all. Of course, my Brummie accent was still with me, plus a couple of the lads I'd been at infants and juniors with were in my class, all of which helped, I think.

Even so, I knew school wasn't for me. It wasn't that I didn't want to learn. I was desperate to learn. It's just school felt stifling and restricting, and they were filling my head with useless information. Would anyone remember Dick Whittington's name if he'd been a good boy and attended school each day? Course not. We only know him because he had the chutzpah to follow his dream. And my dream was still to be a millionaire.

How I'd achieve it was another matter. But I knew I wouldn't find the answer sitting in double geography.

So I went out to work with Dad most days. I really liked it, and he was happy for me to go with him and learn a trade. In his eyes, I was getting a better education with him than I ever would in school.

The only exception to my strict 'No school. They only teach for the masses, and then they want those masses to go out and be employed and get a house they can't afford and struggle to pay their mortgage and get married and have children and go to the pub on a Friday night and have a takeaway on a Saturday and fret about money and wake up one morning on the day they retire from work and think, what was all that about then?' policy was double drama. I figured learning how to stand up in a room full of people and talk confidently was a skill I'd need. Plus, there were fifteen girls and me as the only boy. That was appealing too. I would take the lesson and then sneak out, catching the number 12 bus back home. I don't think anyone missed me, which was either an indication of how the school was run, or my popularity. Both probably.

At home I'd split my time between working with Dad and a weekend job in the greengrocer's six doors down. I was impatient and busy, a heady combination. Then, the day before my sixteenth birthday, I had a rare moment in school and told my form teacher, 'It's my sixteenth birthday tomorrow, so I'm leaving school. This is my last day.'

She said, 'I'm not surprised, but Nick you must come back and take your exams. Okay?'

I smiled, and we both knew I wouldn't.

And that was it. I was a free man; at least, free from school. What I now needed was a plan. Working with Dad was fun, but it wasn't my future.

You know when people say, 'I don't know what it is, but I'll know it when I see it?' Well that's how I felt about my route to wealth. I'd know it when I saw it.

I didn't see it in plumbing.

It wasn't in the greengrocer's either.

However, it might be in my other new venture.

One of the joys of being back with Dad was seeing his parents, my grandma and grandad. I'd missed them so much when I was away with Mum and Ralph. They'd always been so lovely and so supportive, and the first time we went round just days after getting back, Grandma hugged me for so long I began to wonder if she'd ever let go.

Soon after I got back my grandad died, which hit us all hard, especially my grandma. After that, Dad and I would go to her house in Selly Oak whenever we got the chance. She'd make tea for us and make me tell her everything I'd been doing since I saw her last, all before settling down in front of the telly to watch her soaps. Crossroads was her favourite because it was set just outside Birmingham.

Then one week I noticed the telly wasn't on.

'What's up with Crossroads tonight, Grandma?' I said, nodding towards the dark TV in the corner and smiling. 'Have you finally gotten bored with it?'

'It's packed up,' she said, reaching over to pile yet more home-made pie on my plate. 'Eat up, you're a growing lad.'

She was such a good cook. Maybe I should have got her recipes and opened a restaurant, it would have been a lot quicker and a lot easier to make a million and some!

The following morning I asked Dad to stop off at the local electrical shop on our way to work. He guessed what I wanted to do. While the wages from my weekend job in the greengrocer's wasn't much, I'd saved every penny, and when I counted it out, it amounted to fifty pounds. Enough to buy a television.

That night we went back to Grandma's.

'Oh Nick,' she said, squeezing me in another bear hug as we carried the telly into the lounge before unpacking it. 'Thank you. Now, you must let me rent it from you.'

I told her there was no need. But she wouldn't listen.

'No, no. I insist.' She even got the first month out of her purse there and then and handed it over. 'But you will have to come and collect the money each month,' she said, handing over two pounds fifty and barely able to keep the grin from her face.

Dad was smiling too, both of us thinking the same thing, that there were no flies on her! Of course, I realised it was her way of ensuring I visited on a regular basis, which of course I was happy to do.

Anyway, this arrangement had only been going for a short time when Grandma said her next-door neighbour wanted to rent a TV from me too. Apparently, her neighbour, like my grandma, was also in her mid-seventies, had called around to see my nan, seen the TV and asked, 'When did you get the new telly, then?'

My grandma proudly announced that her grandson now rents televisions, and I instantly had my second client. Thankfully, I'd already saved another fifty pounds so was able to buy another and install it.

This felt pretty good for a fifteen-year-old no-hoper. I was now collecting a fiver each month from my rentals, earning around fifteen pounds a week helping Dad and another five from my weekend greengrocer job. So within a couple of weeks I easily had enough to buy another TV as news of my rentals was spreading fast, to the point that I was soon installing two brand-new TVs per month.

By the time my sixteenth birthday came around, the day after I left school, I decided I needed my own transport so I wouldn't have to rely on Dad to taxi me around to collect all the rents.

There was a shop that sold mopeds just down the road, and I had my eye on a really cool one for a while; it was a yellow Yamaha FS1E 50cc. So in I walked, birth certificate in one pocket proving it was my sixteenth birthday and cash in the other. Happy birthday to me.

# Chapter Nine

By the time my seventeenth birthday rolled around, my TV rental operation had twenty customers. That meant I was collecting fifty pounds every month in rent. Quite a considerable sum in the late seventies.

On the actual day of my birthday I took my moped back to the shop from which I bought it and traded it for a 250cc motorbike, the biggest I could legally ride for my age. The power difference was phenomenal, and made me feel like king of the road. Of course, back in those days there weren't so many cars about, and you could be fooled into thinking it was a safer time. And it kind of was, although crashes involving motorbikes were sickeningly common, to the point where they had an advert on TV with the slogan Think Once, Think Twice, Think Bike! showing a car smashing into a man on a motorbike and trapping the rider underneath the bumper while the narrator used his hands to represent a car and bike, one hand flat, the other one balled into a fist, and punched them together to emphasise the point. I always wondered what my grandma thought watching it on one of the TVs rented to her by her biker grandson, but she never mentioned it.

The rule of the road is bikers attract bikers, and whenever we got together we'd swap horror stories of car doors suddenly pinging open from parked cars in front of you, or someone who should have had their eyes tested for driving their car like Mr Magoo.

But I really enjoyed the speed and thrill you get on a motorbike. My best friend at the time, Dave Fortune, also had the same bike, and we would often make our way down to Barmouth at the weekend, leaving early Saturday morning and arriving at around 10am and spending the whole day there before riding back to Brum. It was Dave Fortune who first told me he'd just got a job as a motorcycle courier. I was keen to know more!

Star Wars had just been released, a gallon of four-star petrol was an exorbitant seventy-five pence and the concept of motorbike couriers was in its infancy. The first motorcycle courier firm of any note was called Pony Express and operated out of London. Soon, other firms sprang up, and my mate said he was earning a tidy sum whizzing around the streets of Birmingham delivering small parcels and packages.

That night I told my dad about it. He knew my time working with him was limited, and it wasn't as though I worked with him full-time – there simply wasn't enough demand to keep us both busy. Even so, I felt bad and grabbed us some fish and chips on the way home as a kind of peace offering. However, his reaction was a surprise.

When I told him I was thinking of applying to become a motorcycle courier, he said, 'I think it's a fantastic idea, son. You've gotta go for it!'

I unwrapped my bag and dolloped some ketchup on the side. The chips had gone a bit soggy and the fish was squashed, although it was nothing a good drowning in salt and vinegar couldn't cure. 'You think so?' I said, trying not to feel like I was letting him down.

'I know so,' he said. 'I've always told you, Nick, I can't help you with money or business advice, but what I can give you is a hundred per cent support. I've got your back, son. I think you'd love it, and what's more I think you'd be bloody good at it.'

I don't know what I was expecting. I knew he'd never try and stop me doing anything I really wanted to do, and I knew he'd always support me, but this was the first time I'd ever put it to the test, and I think I felt a bit overwhelmed with just how supportive he was.

'You don't feel like I'm letting you down?'

Face dead serious, he said, 'I never expected you to follow in my footsteps. I think I'd be annoyed if you did. Your dreams are bigger, and I'm proud of you for that.'

So the next day I did the seventies equivalent of drafting a CV, writing a covering letter and applying for a job interview, which was going down there and knocking on the door. Leg power and gumption my grandma called it.

The company was called Despatch Riders, and the man in charge didn't seem in the least bit surprised to have me knock on the door and ask, 'Any jobs going?' I added, 'My mate Dave Fortune already works for you so I know what's involved.'

'I presume you've got a motorbike?' he said.

I half smiled; isn't that a given? And nodded.

Reading my expression, he said, 'Oh, you'd be surprised. Is that it outside?'

He was standing by the front window looking out. I'd parked and chained it up, having first made sure it was spotlessly clean.

'That's it,' I confirmed, unsure if I was meant to join him or remain where I was standing.

He nodded approvingly. 'Okay, job's yours,' he said, and I wondered who he was offering the position to, me or the bike. But either way, I was now a fully fledged motorcycle courier, and it felt great. The deal was, I'd be self-employed and would be given a share of the jobs as and when they came in.

The company was run by Phil and his sleeping partner Norman, whom I never met, and for six months I would dash around on my motorbike delivering bits and bobs to firms up and down Birmingham, and without even knowing it I got an understanding of how a courier company operated.

Then, one night when Dad and I were sitting in our favourite spots in the lounge – Dad closest to the TV, me a little way over from him – I found I couldn't concentrate, could hardly sit still. He'd never upgraded the furniture from the days when he and Mum were together, so everything was a bit old and saggy, but super comfortable because of it, so sitting still was never normally an issue.

'How's work?' he asked. He knew something was up, of course he did.

I shrugged. 'Busy. Crazy busy. I didn't even have time to stop for lunch today. None of us did. And they're advertising for more riders.'

'Sounds like they're onto a good little number.'

I responded with an 'Mmm.' Outside, the kettle did its thing in the kitchen to alert us that it had, in fact, boiled. Neither of us moved.

'I've been thinking,' I said. 'I mean, a courier company. How hard can it be? You get a call, you go and collect a parcel from one place and drop it off at another. Then you bill the customer. It's not rocket science.'

Ladies and gentleman, may I present to you this year's winner of Understatement of the Year, in the category of, Bloody Fool who hasn't a clue of what he's talking about, I give you… It's Nick Terry! Okay that didn't go off in my mind, but it should have. Sure I had the fundamentals down, just as someone else might sum up space travel as 'You build a vehicle that can go really fast, really high, and you strap yourself in.' What neither statement acknowledges are the nuances. The details that will make or break your project. But I was a kid, and I still had this unshakable belief that somehow I was going to be a huge success.

Intuition was always one of my dad's strongest traits. He got up and I thought he was heading for the kitchen to fix us teas, but instead he made his way over to the telly and turned the volume down. Then he turned to me, nodded and said, 'Go on…'

I hadn't quite formulated in my mind what I meant exactly, and the fact he wanted me to expand on it made me nervous. He was looking at me, and it kind of made me focus my thoughts, realising that, more than anything else, I wanted to know his opinion. So I told him everything I'd been thinking; how I could see me running a little courier company for myself, and if I undercut all the competition by a penny a mile, I could see how I'd get customers.

'Do it,' he said. 'You've got nothing to lose and everything to gain. You're young and ambitious. You'll smash it, son.'

Dinner now done, I balled up what was left of the fish and chips, which was most of it, in the wrapper and tossed it on the table for Dad to take out later – I might have been a budding entrepreneur, but I was still seventeen.

Sitting back, I said, 'I don't know. I'm going to need some money to get started. Not much, but some.'

'Fine. I'll buy your TV rentals from you. You won't have much time for it anyway, not once you start.'

He offered me £500, which was more than it was worth. The next day I also sold my motorbike and bought a Mark II Ford Escort, and quit my job.

This was it. This was really it.

Sourcing a quick, cheap printing service, I used some of the money to get business cards, flyers, leaflets and a small black and white brochure printed that I sent out to all the clients I knew had used my old firm, Despatch Riders. The balance, what there was of it, was used for cash flow.

With a few simple maps pinned up on my bedroom wall, and a phone wired from the downstairs of our little terraced house, I had my first office. Birmingham Express Couriers, later to become BXT Couriers Limited, was born.

# Chapter Ten

One of the very first jobs I had was to deliver a small parcel from a company called Sans Serif to Centre One Advertising Ltd based over in Knowle, just outside Solihull.

The chap had specifically requested a motorcycle as this was an urgent delivery. In those very early days, it was just me on my own, so I would take the phone off the hook (far better to be engaged than just ringing out), and would carry out the deliveries myself. This job would be about a twenty-mile round trip and should only take about an hour. I also knew Centre One Advertising was not an easy place to find, having made a few deliveries there before when I was working for my old company.

When I arrived at Sans Serif, the chap took one look at me and said, 'Oh, you're not on a bike then?'

Thinking on my feet, I said, 'No, sorry, all the bikes were out and I'm the nearest person available.'

Nodding in understanding, if not delight, he said, 'Thing is, it's not an easy place to find. And it's very urgent.'

In my most calm, professional tone, I said, 'Oh don't worry, I know where it is, just off the A4141 Warwick Road on the right, just before the traffic island, and their driveway is next to the phone box. Right?'

Surprised, he confirmed, 'Yes, that's right.'

It's not often I get to show off, so I added, 'It's the house that's been converted into offices.'

This really brought a smile to his face, and he was clearly reassured I knew exactly where I was going.

The second I was out of his vision, I ran like a gang of skinheads were chasing me, jumped into my car and took off into the line of traffic. If I could get there quickly, this could really be a good contract.

Zipping in and out of the cars around me, I drove like a legend and made it there so fast I'd challenge any biker to do it quicker. Okay, look, I'm not proud of my driving that day. I didn't just break a few road laws, I practically obliterated The Highway Code, but I was desperate, Your Honour.

As soon as I arrived at the delivery point, I asked if I could use their phone and called Sans Serif to say the package was delivered. My man was delighted.

The next day I had another call from Sans Serif, with yet another delivery to the same place. The chap on the phone said, 'Can you please make sure you send a bike this time?'

'Yes of course!' I said, swiftly taking the phone off the hook, grabbing my old leather jacket and crash helmet, which thankfully I still had, and raced out the door.

Parking my car around the corner, I donned my jacket and helmet and walked into their office. 'Don't worry, I know where it is,' I said breezily, grabbing the parcel on the side and strolling back out before they could say anything.

It was while racing over to Centre One for a second time in as many days that I had to smile to myself. They thought there were at least three people who worked for this new Birmingham Express outfit. There's the nice chap who answers the phone, the smart guy in the car, and the motorcycle courier who clearly knows where he's going. I was of course playing the role of all three. It was some ten years later, having got to know the owner of Sans Serif really well, a lovely chap called Eddy, that I told him the story.

After a few weeks of setting up Birmingham Express, I was in a position to employ a few motorcycle riders. In fact, I didn't really employ them as they were all self-employed owner riders. Now we have companies like Uber, Just Eat and Amazon that do the same. The advantage was that if I wasn't busy, I wasn't paying any wages. The disadvantage was I had less control over when they would be available to work, which meant the majority of jobs went to my number one employee, who ran around on two little legs pistoning like a sewing machine in an electric surge. Me! I realised early on that for my company to succeed it was going to take a combination of hard work and luck, but mainly sheer graft.

I got lucky early on with a company called Force Ten Couriers. This company had set up their business a couple of months after me and it was growing rapidly. It was owned by a man who also ran a freight business, and he was often asked if he could deliver small packages, so he thought he would set up a courier company to run alongside.

Force Ten was managed day-to-day by Terry Warilow. One day he called to ask if I had a courier that could cover a job as all his own riders were out on other work. I was of course delighted to help, and we ended up sub-contracting the odd job here and there to help each other out. Much better to sub-contract a job than turn work away.

Terry became my go-to when work got crazy and I couldn't rustle up one more rider.

Reaching for the phone I dialled his number. 'Terry? It's Nick. Don't suppose you can help with a job, can you?'

'Hang on, Nick,' he said, and put his hand over the receiver, which is what we used to do when putting people on hold. When he came back, he said, 'Sorry about that. Yes, no problem. But it's going to be the last time, I'm afraid.'

'Last time? Why, what's happened?'

'We're closing.'

By all accounts, his boss, who I had never met, was closing down the business as it was just not viable or profitable enough for him. I suppose when running a freight company turning over a million a year, a small courier company turning over a few hundred pounds a week was nothing more than a distraction.

Terry said he was about to throw out some of his sales brochures, as they were not going to be of any use to them. He wondered if I wanted them. 'Maybe you could put a sticker over the phone number? Either way, they're free if they're any use to you.'

The following morning I went to Terry's office in Thorp Street, which was virtually in the centre of Birmingham, and met Terry for the first time. Up until then we had only ever spoken on the phone.

Terry was a good guy, the type of person you feel as though you've known for years on the first meeting. He showed me the pile of brochures that he had stacked up in the corner.

When I had printed my own 'point of sale' literature I could only afford to have a couple of hundred printed, and they were in black and white. Here Terry had what must have been over a thousand colour brochures.

'Crikey, Terry,' I said. 'It would be cheaper for me move into these offices than have a thousand stickers with my phone number printed.'

'Well, they're becoming free. I'm moving out on Friday,' he replied.

It was a light-bulb moment and a bit of luck that everyone needs in business from time to time. My turnover at the time was about £200 per week, which was still not bad for a lad working from his bedroom. Force Ten's turnover, I was told by Terry, was nearer £300 per week, so overnight I had the opportunity to more than double my turnover.

Terry's office was set up much better than mine, with various maps on the wall placed in metal frames. Small magnetic discs were strategically placed on the maps indicating where each courier was at any one time. Each courier was given a number and this number was written on the disc. This idea of allocating each courier with their own number was used throughout the whole time I ran my business. It always made me smile when I would overhear someone asking, 'Where's Jim 50?' or 'When will Richard 12 be back?'

Compared to what I had back in my office/bedroom, this was a slick operation. In addition to Terry's office, which doubled up as the 'control room', there was also a small room next door for the couriers to wait for their next job, and a hatch between the two offices to pass the job sheets across.

I asked Terry to see if his boss would be interested in selling me the name and goodwill of Force Ten, and if so, for how much? I also asked if he could check with the landlord if they would be happy for me to take over the lease to the offices.

This was my first acquisition, one of three I made in total, and cost me £1,000. A lot of money, and it took all the working capital I had left. But this was too good an opportunity to turn down. The landlords were happy for me to take over the rent, so Birmingham Express and Force Ten united.

From bedroom to a proper company, with proper offices, in a few short months. Dick Whittington would have been proud. My dad certainly was.

# Chapter Eleven

The night I signed the lease to take over the offices at Thorp Street was a Friday night, the date I will never forget – Friday 27th October 1978. My little company, which I started on 1st July 1978 was still only four months old and I had made my first acquisition. Turnover was now £500 per week and I was still only eighteen years old.

That night, when I got home, I had tea with Dad the same as always. There was no champagne, no fanfare, just me and Dad sitting in our spots on the sofa. Minder was on the TV, a show about two loveable rogues, one hiring out the other as a bodyguard. Normally I'd lose myself in the programme, but not tonight.

I kept thinking over and over again – from tomorrow I'd have to make the offices pay. They'd have to work. It felt like the big time. I didn't know whether to feel terrified or elated, so I kind of swung between the two.

On the telly the bodyguard on the show was called Terry. Terry McCann and Arthur Daley. The plots weren't difficult to follow, and distracted as I was, I still knew what was going on. Then I had the weirdest thought. I wished I had a Terry. Not the bodyguard stuff, but someone who had my back no matter what. That sense that someone was there for me, that I wasn't quite so alone.

I looked across at Dad. I loved him and he was always there for me, but this felt bigger somehow. Scarier. More to lose if it went wrong.

'You not going to finish your tea, son?' Dad said.

He'd cooked the tea that night, which is another way of saying he'd opened a can of beans and buttered the toast.

Peering down at my plate, I realised I'd just been shifting it about. I kind of felt hungry, but I think the impact of what I'd done was starting to sink in. 'No. Sorry, Dad. Bit distracted, you know?'

Smiling at me, he returned his attention to the telly.

The following morning, even though it was Saturday, I got up before six, dressed in a sharp light grey suit and left for my new office. At that time in the morning it was a doddle to park, and I walked the short distance along the pavement to the outer door, a big black affair with the number 37 printed on it. To the side was a list of companies that had offices within the building. About eight I guess. Once inside, to the left was a stack of post boxes, each with a business card sellotaped to the corresponding box. All bar one, mine, and I made a mental note to attach one just as soon as I had them printed.

Ahead were the stairs, which were very steep and went straight up to a large landing on the first floor. Here, immediately to the right under a wooden overhang were three black dustbins for the use of the tenants. Also on this floor were the communal toilets.

On the first floor there were about five offices. You had to walk through numerous doors and corridors to find mine. It was all a bit dark and spooky.

On the very top floor was a dance studio. I was later to find out it was run by two old dears who would turn up every Wednesday afternoon to open it up. I would then hear the music and I assume pensioners shuffling around doing the waltz. I really didn't mind. It was nice to have some company because it could often be very quiet and eerie at times, especially at night. A lot of the offices were left unoccupied, with owners only coming back to check post, make a few phone calls and then return to whatever they were doing before.

Letting myself in, I closed the door behind me and breathed in. I was to discover the whole block was cleaned once a week by someone with shares in a bleach factory. If it had a surface, horizontal, vertical, metal, glass or mirror, it got a wipe over with a bleach-soaked rag or mop. It made the whole block smell a bit like a swimming pool, but with the door closed behind me I had a really strong feeling that these offices were mine. Nick Terry, you little beauty, you're in business my friend.

It was so exciting having my own proper office, but now the first thing I needed to do was find the kettle. For the bargain price of £1,000, not only had I bought the goodwill and client list of Force Ten Couriers but I had also acquired all their furniture, stationery, maps… in fact, everything. I don't think even Arthur Daley could have done better.

The second thing I needed to figure out was what to do with the stack of brochures piled in the corner. Thankfully, now that I had taken over the offices of Force Ten, and with that their phone number, I didn't need to change anything on the brochures. I had already called each and every one of my clients the week before to inform them that as from Saturday 28th October there would be a new number to call.

Having had a good walk around my new offices and looked in every nook and cranny, I then sat down at my new desk and spent the morning addressing hundreds of envelopes and inserting my newly acquired brochures and leaflets. When my hand ached from writing and my eyes squinted from reading the yellow pages, I'd stop for ten minutes, walk about, then go back to it. I worked long into the afternoon and knew I would be back on Sunday to complete the task.

Little by little work began to increase, both new and old customers booking couriers every day. I was clearly busy with both the work coming in for Force Ten and my old established customers, but I still wanted more.

Beside the phone I kept a pad to jot down customer instructions for a job when I was lucky, or a quote when I wasn't. From these hastily written notes I'd later write up the work or type out the quote on Mum's manual typewriter, which thankfully she had not taken with her when she left Dad.

Using it would make me think of my mum; she used to use this typewriter to type out Dad's invoices. How did Dad manage after she had gone? I should have asked him but I never did.

I hadn't thought about Mum since I'd left, over three years ago now. I had made no attempt to contact her, or, I guess, her me. I would pause, sitting still in the office, just listening, thinking, my mind now racing – and how was Fred, my dog? God, I missed him so much it hurt, really hurt. I certainly missed him more than Mum, which I guess spoke volumes. Why did she never try to contact me? But my thoughts went immediately back to Fred. Was he okay? Were they looking after him, walking him? Fussing him and playing with him like I used to do? As a tear ran down my cheek I stopped myself; let it go, Nick, concentrate, head down, move on, focus, work to be done, and anyway, you have no time for these sort of thoughts.

Giving myself a talking to was going to be a regular occurrence in my life from now on.

Snapping out of it and flicking back through the pad looking at all the quotes I'd given that day, I suddenly had an idea. If I wrote down all the notes and quotes on a scrap piece of paper, it stood to reason everybody did.

Looking at my watch, I noted it was seven thirty in the evening, long after business hours had finished. Grabbing my suit jacket, I locked up and drove my car to my competitors, Despatch Riders, where I used to work, parked down the street and walked back, taking care to make sure no lights were on with someone working late. They weren't.

I knew, of course, where their little squat metal bins with metal lids were to be found, outside in a little courtyard, no fence, no gates, this was going to be easy. After a little rooting around, I found that the bins contained the usual pile of used teabags, half-eaten sandwiches, the odd apple core, but the real gold I was looking for were all the rough scrawled notes of the telephone conversations they'd had for the past few days. It was a goldmine of work and quotes and even included the prices they'd quoted. Gathering as many as I could, I made good and left. The following morning I hit the phone.

'Ah yes, good morning, can I speak to Mr Richardson please? Hi, my name is Nick Terry from Birmingham Express Couriers. I'm just calling to introduce myself and my company in case you're ever in need of a reliable courier, and to tell you our competitive rates are...' At this point I'd glance down at the paper I'd pulled out and unravelled from the bins, subtract ten per cent, and hey presto, a very competitive price was offered. It didn't always work, but it did sometimes. To this day I'm very mindful of what I chuck out.

On top of this I was continually sending out the flyers and leaflets to various companies regularly trying to drum up new business, and the procurement department at British Leyland, with its main plant in Longbridge, Northfield, Birmingham received one of my flyers.

At its height, BL was employing around 200,000 people, 25,000 of them at the Longbridge plant alone. BL was producing cars with very famous brand names, such as Mini, Austin, Jaguar, Land Rover, Triumph and Rover.

However, the build quality was often in doubt and the efficiency of the various plants was very poor compared with present automotive production lines. One of the new cars about to be launched, and rumoured as being break or bust for BL, was the new Mini Metro.

BL had a large test track and testing facility in a place called Gaydon in Warwickshire, which is about twenty-five miles south of Birmingham. The new Mini Metro was being put through its final testing before launch. One day, out of the blue, I took a call from a Mr Taylor, who was from the procurement department at BL, asking me if we could send a courier every day to Gaydon to pick up some important papers. These papers were the daily report on how the new car was performing. Nowadays they would be emailed across, but in 1979 not even fax machines were widely used.

At three on the dot every day, a courier would arrive at the gatehouse at Gaydon Test Centre, collect a large bundle of highly confidential papers and deliver these straight to the procurement department back at their head offices.

I was delighted to get my first contract and soon discovered having regular bookings, as opposed to one-off deliveries, was going to be the way forward. My only big concern with this contract was that BL was notorious for being slow payers, and I worried about my cash flow. Before the commencement of this contract, I was brave enough to tactfully air this concern to Mr Taylor and thankfully he fully understood. He said he would arrange for payment of my monthly invoice to be given from petty cash. My petty cash tin had a float of £25; my invoice to BL was going to be around £400. I wondered how they could pay that much from petty cash, and smiled.

The contract went well, and before I knew it, four weeks had passed, my invoices had been sent and I was thinking it might be time for me to ask for payment. I was paying my couriers weekly, so cash flow was getting somewhat tight and £400 would make a big difference to me.

I was nearing the point of picking up the phone to Mr Taylor when he beat me to it. Only, he didn't use the phone.

I opened the door on the second knock, expecting to see one of the couriers back from a job, but instead, a very smart, tall guy, mid-fifties in a well-fitted suit stood in the doorway. He had an air of importance about him that made me nervous. I of course knew instantly who is was.

'Hello, can I help you?'

'Yes, I'm looking for Mr Terry,' he said, peering over my shoulder.

'You've found him.'

Giving me a smile, he said, 'No, I think it's your father I might be looking for, Nick Terry?'

'Yes, that's me,' I replied. 'Are you Mr Taylor by any chance?'

There was a long pause while he looked me up and down, clearly assessing the situation. 'Nick Terry,' he said. 'Oh right, it's just I was expecting someone older. Is this your business then?'

We were still on the doorstep, and I had a feeling I knew what was coming; he wasn't going to be happy giving me this business now he realised the company was run by a young whippersnapper of a kid. There was no point lying and nothing I could do but admit that, yes, I was Nick Terry.

Another short pause and then he walked straight towards me, put out his hand, shook mine with great enthusiasm and said these words that I will never forget. 'God, I wish my son would get off his arse and do something like you're doing… well done, lad!'

I invited him in and he wanted to know all about how I started the business, and we chatted for over an hour in my little office. Just as he was leaving, he asked if he could take a handful of my leaflets to distribute around the factory and into various offices.

Within two weeks of that meeting I was working for BL's accounts, marketing and sales departments, with a lot more work from the procurement department and many other departments besides. Soon my monthly invoices shot up to almost a thousand pounds a month, a small fortune in my eyes, and they could no longer be paid by petty cash. But, I was promised, I wouldn't be kept waiting, and I wasn't. All because the guy with enough clout to matter, one Mr Taylor, had marked my company as the preferred option.

When the first cheque for a grand came in, I sat at my desk and held it in my hands, marvelling at the numbers. One thousand pounds. I couldn't keep the grin from my face. 'Terry,' I said out loud in my best Minder imitation of Arthur Daily's voice, 'take the night off, son. I don't need ya, I'm doing just fine on my own,' and I rushed out to bank it.

# Chapter Twelve

Skip forward a year. The business is thriving, I've got an assistant working with me and a full-on team of self-employed couriers at my disposal. One day, a client, a small advertising firm based just off Five Ways Island near Edgbaston, telephoned requesting a courier.

Graham Rote & Co would call at least once a day requesting a motorcycle courier to take documents to a firm of printers, or maybe a draft copy of advertising to be zipped over to one of their clients.

So it wasn't at all unusual to get a call from them requesting a courier to take a recording of a tape to a commercial radio station in Derby. They explained it was an advert that was due to be broadcast just before the three o'clock news. Given it was already gone eleven, we had to get our skates on.

It got top priority, and I assured Sarah, who had made the call, that a courier would be with her to collect the package within the next ten minutes. From there it should be in Derby a couple of hours later. I gave her a delivery time of around one, leaving plenty of time for them to make the broadcasting slot at three.

The next courier available was Dave. He was around twenty-five years old and had been working for me for about a year. I explained the importance of this job to him, but given he rode a Honda 500, we both felt the delivery deadline was not going to be an issue.

Back then there were no satnavs, mobile phones or even pagers. When Dave left the office, I had no way of contacting him, or vice versa. If he needed to call in, he would have to find a phone box or ask the receptionists at the point of delivery if he could use their phone.

I thought no more about the job until Sarah rang at around quarter to one, asking if I'd heard anything from the courier as he had still not arrived. I said I hadn't, but I assured her he was probably only a few minutes away.

Half an hour later Sarah was back on the phone saying the courier had still not arrived, and she was now being told by the radio company that they had to have it in the next ten minutes if it was to be broadcast. I had still not heard from Dave, who would normally have called me if he was having any problems.

'Sarah, honestly I've heard nothing, so I can only guess he's minutes away,' I assured her. But in truth I was starting to pace the office.

I was well aware reputation was everything. You could make a hundred deliveries for a company without any issues, but one late delivery and that's all they will remember. In this business, you really were only as good as your last job. Graham Rote & Co was a good client and I definitely did not want to lose their business.

Striding a trench in the carpet of my office, I tried to send Dave telepathic messages to contact me – it was the only communication we had, and it never worked.

Two o'clock passed and still no sign of Dave. Sarah called and told me she had just been informed by the radio station that it was now too late to make the afternoon slot, and at best it would go out the following day. To say she was not happy was an understatement. All I could do was apologise profusely and promise I would let her know as soon as I heard anything.

'I'm sure there must be a good reason. Dave's one of my best guys.'

She said, 'Yeah. Sure. Good.' She sounded distracted and annoyed, leaving me in no doubt I'd lost the business.

The trench in the carpet felt like it was getting deeper and deeper as I continued worry-walking back and forth. Where the heck was Dave? This was so out of character. Normally giving a job to him was as safe as knocking on wood.

The phone ringing brought me to my senses and probably saved the last threads of the carpet. As I answered it, a friendly voice on the other end said, 'Hey, Nick.'

It was Robert. I had met him in a second-hand record shop about a year earlier and we had become good friends. We got chatting and it turned out he worked for a successful media agency, and they often used taxis to move documents around the country.

'That's a coincidence,' I said brightly.

He looked questioningly at me.

'I run a courier firm.'

Robert worked for a high profile Midlands based media company that looked after the interests of a number of high profile people in radio and television. People like Ed Doolan, Les Ross, Tony Butler, Nick Owen, Anne Diamond and Larry Grayson. Robert had very kindly introduced me to some of them, and as a young nineteen-year-old, I was in awe of them.

I had assumed Robert had just phoned to book a courier, but instead he asked, 'Are you okay?'

'I'm fine,' I lied. Then I took a deep sigh and said, 'Well, it's one of those days, you know? One of my guys is late on an important delivery, and I think I've lost the client over it.'

Silence for one, two, three seconds. Then he said, 'You don't know. You haven't heard.'

They weren't questions, more statements, but I answered anyway. 'Heard what?'

Again a couple of seconds' silence. Then, taking control, he said, 'Okay, I want you to leave the office. Walk straight over towards my office and I'm coming now to meet you halfway. Don't ask any questions, just do it and do it now. I'll see you in five.' And the phone went down.

So I did. I asked someone else to take over the phones and walked outside. I don't know what I was thinking. I'm not sure I was capable of thinking anything. I know my breathing was tight and my legs felt heavy, but I made them walk in the right direction.

The first thing I thought when Robert pulled up next to me in his car was, you cheated, I thought you were going to be walking too. Leaning across, he opened the passenger door and I climbed in.

With a hand over my face I uttered the only word that would come out, 'What?'

'Not here.' Aiming the car into the line of traffic, he said, 'I'm looking after the keys to a friend's house. It's empty.'

I closed my eyes, my stomach somersaulting.

Letting us in, he plonked me on the sofa and left to fix us some teas. Dread was making me feel sick. This was not good. This was really, really not good.

Walking in and handing me a mug, he said quietly, 'Sarah called me.'

Startled, I said, 'Sarah? Sarah from Graham Rote's?'

He nodded, explaining that they knew one another well. 'Nick, she was in bits, sobbing, not making an awful lot of sense, but, eventually, she said she'd persuaded a courier to go quickly to deliver a package to a Derby radio station and they had just called her to say the package was eventually delivered by a police motorcyclist. He had found the package in the rear box of a motorcycle, and the motorcyclist had been involved in a tragic accident. The policeman had taken it upon himself to complete the delivery.'

I couldn't think. I'm not sure I could breathe. All I could think was, Jesus Christ, not Dave. No, no, no, not Dave. Please not Dave.

'Sarah's boss had to call her husband to come and pick her up,' he continued.

Robert asked which courier firm she had used, and when she replied Birmingham Express, he'd phoned me.

It felt like my world had ended. All I could see was Dave's face, smiling, reassuring. 'Yeah boss, don't worry. I'll get it there,' were his last words, and they repeated in my head like some macabre mantra.

I spent the next awful hour crying, panicking, shouting but mainly sobbing. I was a wreck, and it was only Robert's calmness that stopped me from completely losing it. I decided there and then that I would have to close down the business. That was it. There was no way I could continue. I was truly in pieces.

Calling his office an hour later to say he wouldn't be coming back for the rest of the day, Robert suddenly turned and looked me straight in the eyes. I only heard one side of the conversation, but it was enough.

# Chapter Thirteen

Robert, his face stern and serious, said into the phone, 'Are you sure?' Silence for a beat. Then, 'Yep, I understand. Just to be certain, you're absolutely one hundred per cent sure? Okay. Yep. And which hospital is he in? Of course, he's with me now. Yes, he's fine.' He glanced at me, his face contorting in a way that meant I probably didn't look fine. Then switching back he said, 'Has anyone let Sarah know? Good, how was she?' A snort, his eyes flicking to the ceiling. 'I bet she did. Okay, thank you. Yes, I'll tell him now.'

Have you ever seen a bouncy castle deflate, when all the sides sag in and the middle becomes soft and spongy? That's exactly how I felt. Dave was going to be okay.

Oh my God, Dave was going to be okay.

It's so weird. Before I'd experienced it for real, if you'd told me about the seismic shift in emotion from 'Your man's dead' to 'Oh wait... no, he's going to be just fine', I'd have said I'd be jumping up and down in ecstasy. But in reality all I could do was sag, and that was an effort.

Robert made a few more calls, just to be certain. One was to the hospital, who confirmed Dave had suffered a broken leg, cuts and bruises, but otherwise was fine.

We later found out a car had pulled out in front of him. Dave wasn't speeding. The driver had simply not seen him. An ambulance and the police were called to the scene. Dave had managed to speak to one of the officers and said he had a package in his top box that was destined for Radio Derby. The police motorcyclist told him not to worry, he would ensure it got there.

When he arrived at Radio Derby and handed it over to the receptionist, she looked him up and down, more than a little surprised that a policeman was delivering the package, and said, 'Um. Wow. I don't understand. Yes, we've been waiting for it, I'll let them know it's here, but…'

Without adding any drama, as if you needed to, the policeman explained that the courier had been involved in a serious accident. The receptionist passed the package up the line together with the story, which, as it does, became a little more sensational each time it was repeated. By the time it had done the rounds and someone had called Sarah in Birmingham to say they had the tape, it had become a fatal accident.

'I need to go and see him,' I announced, my mind sending signals to my arms and legs to do their thing and get me up off the sofa. In normal circumstances you take for granted the cooperation of one's limbs, and their refusal to obey commands comes as quite a shock.

'I don't think so,' Robert said, watching me still flopped out on the sofa. 'You need something to eat first. Get some energy back into you.'

'I'm not hungry,' I said, still marvelling at how the human body can override direct instructions and impose a full-body shutdown when it feels you need time to come to terms with a dramatic shock.

'I don't care,' Robert continued. 'You're not going anywhere without something inside you.'

'No really. I'm not hungry.'

Taking a second to look me up and down, he said, 'When was the last time you ate?'

I couldn't think. There were always people around at the office, so I couldn't eat there. At home there was Dad. I remembered getting a sandwich in my car and parking up, but there were people walking by. It's really hard to be by yourself.

'I don't know, but it's not important,' I said.

'You look thin.'

Suddenly I could feel my legs and arms power up once more. Houston, we have regained control. With that I got up.

I drove to the Royal Derby Hospital that night to check on Dave. He looked worse than he sounded and was discharged the following day. He eventually returned to work, but from then on in the office as my first ever branch manager rather than out on the road.

Robert, Sarah, and I all met for dinner a few weeks later. Sarah had no idea that her best friend knew me; it really is a small world. We chatted and ate and drank, and kind of debriefed. It felt good to get it all out. Cathartic.

I could feel Robert watching me eat. Could feel his eyes on me every time I raised my fork. It made me feel prickly and uncomfortable and a bit panicked. I forced myself to have three mouthfuls, excused myself, went to the loos and made myself sick.

It was a few days later that Graham Rote called again to say they had another parcel that they needed delivering but it was too big to go on a bike, and they wondered if I had any vans?

So, I hadn't lost their business after all. Phew! Okay, vans. No I didn't, but I wasn't going to tell them that. Thinking quick, I said, 'Oh yes,' figuring my next call would be to a hire company.

The second I put down the phone I opened the hatch that separated my office from the pool of drivers and yelled, 'Can anyone drive a van?'

The following day they called again, once more asking for a van. They did it every day for the next four weeks. The invoice from the hire company at the end of the month almost made my eyes pop out. It was massive. At this rate it would be cheaper to buy one. So I did, and even had it sign-written. Then I employed my first driver and put him on the cards.

Within days other clients were phoning to say they had seen my van out and about and booked it for work, saying they hadn't realised that I provided a van service. More vans were acquired, each one signed with the company's logo, and as the business grew, so did the demand for more vans and drivers. Within four months of Dave's accident I didn't have a single motorcycle courier on my books.

I liked looking out the window and watching my vans pull up or drive away. It gave me a sense of inner well-being, like I was on the right path. Don't get me wrong, I was grafting to keep them all going, pulling hours that would make a junior doctor flinch. But it was going in the right direction. Of course, the other reason I liked looking out the window was the girl from the bank who walked by every afternoon. Come on, I was only twenty after all.

We had a game, this beauty and I. At five thirty each night I'd stand at the window and she'd come around the corner into view, glancing up to make sure I was watching her. I always was. Then I'd see her smile, and I'd do the same. It felt like we shared this secret little moment together. Something special just for us. And she was hot. I'm talking wow hot. In business, body language is something you have to learn. It's one of the keys to success, and I was getting pretty good at it. But body language in girls was still a mystery to me. For instance, after she glanced up and made sure I was watching her, she'd cross her arms under her ample boobs. She did this every time. It was clearly a trick, but why? Was she reassuring herself? Was she teasing? Or was it something else? I had no idea, and it wasn't like I could ask anyone. That's one of the problems when you're a teenage boss in a firm full of grown men: who can you turn to for general life questions? What was I supposed to do, shout into the pool of couriers, 'Hey, Steve, can you pick up from Edgbaston and deliver to Northfield? Oh, and by the way, how can you tell if a girl likes you?'

It was also no coincidence that she worked at the bank I used. Her name was Diane.

Whenever I went to pay in the cheques or get a little cash out to top up my rather small petty cash float, I always stood in line hoping that her till window would become vacant. Usually, I would end up at Pam's window, who, while also being lovely, was in her late fifties and would talk me to death along with other customers. She would want to know what I had been up to and took a genuine interest in my growing business.

One day, Diane was nowhere to been seen, and I ended up at Gwen's window, another one of the cashiers. When she handed back my paying-in book I noticed she had slipped a bit of paper inside. This wasn't a twenty-pound note, but something more exciting. Gwen was having a house party at the weekend and inside my paying-in book was an invite.

I knew Diane was going to be there. This was my chance.

# Chapter Fourteen

I hadn't been to a party in forever. My life just hadn't evolved that way. Actually, wait, that's not true. Evolution had nothing to do with it. It was a conscious decision. I think I decided very early on that I had a choice to either live the life of a regular teenager or fight for my company and success. And the latter felt bigger, more urgent somehow. I didn't dwell on it, but scrunched away in the back of my mind I knew how many hours I was putting in each week. Seventy, eighty maybe. On occasions, probably more. I even had a pager that pinged messages from an outside company with any night-time calls that would go off at all hours.

Weekends were the same. On Saturdays I was in the office catching up on paperwork, including typing out the week's invoices. On Sundays, I would drive down to London making deliveries for WH Smith Do It All, whose administration office at that time was in Dudley, about ten miles north-east of Birmingham.

The thought of leading a regular life alongside this was impossible. Yet I couldn't get this girl who walked past my window each afternoon, and worked in the bank, out of my head.

Actually, I felt terrified walking up to the front door of the party. My comfort zone had become my work, and this was so far removed it felt almost overwhelming. I'd even had to buy some new clothes, as the only things I ever wore were suits, and not even I could rock up to a shindig in a two-piece, shirt and tie.

I knocked on the door and Gwen answered, a cheeky grin plastered across her face when she saw who it was.

'I knew you'd come,' she said, ushering me in. 'I told them you would. She's in there.'

Was it that obvious?

I walked into the front room to be confronted by all the professional staff at the bank looking chilled, relaxed and slightly pissed. I was handed a drink and told where the food was. God, can you imagine eating anything in front of all these people? I'd rather die.

Then I spotted Diane, and we were skilfully on-purpose/not-on-purpose manoeuvred next to one another. Until now the only thing we'd ever spoken about was paying in cheques. Looking at her and smiling, I said, 'You walk past my office on your way home each night,' which sounded far creepier than I intended.

She laughed, arched an eyebrow and said, 'Do I?'

God she was amazing. She had on an all-in-one blue trouser suit, her dark curly hair pinned up on one side with a matching slide, and a gold neckless around her neck that sparkled whenever she moved. I could not take my eyes off her.

Luckily, she didn't seem to mind.

'They tease me about you,' she said.

'Who do?'

After shrugging and taking a sip of wine, she said, 'All of them. They've been hatching all sorts of plans to get us together.'

'Have they now.' With some effort I looked away from her and glanced around the room. There weren't just people from the bank there, but you could spot the ones that were as they all suddenly looked away from us like poor spies on their first surveillance.

'See?' she said. 'Just the fact that we're talking will fuel the office gossip for a month. Do you want to get something to eat?'

NO. 'Sure!'

And that was it. This sexy, gorgeous, confident woman became my girlfriend.

Until she wasn't.

Meanwhile, Birmingham Express had moved from being a small motorcycle courier company to van couriers. The extra work meant our meagre offices were now bulging.

My landlords, Birmingham Anglers Association, who had kindly allowed me to take over the lease, had their offices on the ground floor.

On the first day of every month I would knock and hand over a cheque for the next month's rent. I was never late paying, ever.

Strolling along the bleach-scented corridor, cheque in hand, I spotted Brian ahead of me walking up and down muttering to himself. He looked like an extra from One Flew Over The Cuckoo's Nest. Brian was the company secretary at Birmingham Anglers and my contact to pay the rent to. He was a smart man, well-spoken, and normally had it together.

'Brian, are you okay?' I said, approaching. His behaviour was well out of character and clearly he was agitated about something.

'Keys. Damn keys. Can't think how it happened. Aye? What? Oh, it's you. End of the month is it?' he said, glancing down at the cheque still in my hand.

Putting two and two together, I said, 'Office or car?'

He looked at me like I was the mad one. That made me laugh. 'You've lost your keys. Are they for your office or your car?'

'Oh! Yes I have! My car. I thought I might have dropped them in the hallway out here, but there's no sign of them anywhere. I guess I must have lost them outside somewhere. On the pavement maybe.'

'Have you not got a spare set?' I asked, trying to be helpful but not sure my question was of much use.

'Yes. At home,' he said, his tone now agitated and snappy.

Then it dawned on me that actually I could be of some help. 'Well, I could send a courier to collect them, as long as someone was there to hand them over.'

Visibly relaxing, he said, 'Can you do that? My wife is there. I could call her to say someone will collect them?'

'Of course,' I said brightly.

'Hum, how much is this going to cost me?'

Shrugging, I asked where he lived. He told me, and it wasn't far. Figuring it was always a good thing to keep one's landlord on your side, I dashed a hand through the air in the universal sign for 'get out of here'.

'Really? Gosh, that's very kind of you.'

From that moment on we became firm friends, and it was shortly after he gave me the heads-up that one of the companies above me, in a much bigger set of offices, was moving out, and if I was interested he'd give me a good deal on the rent.

I desperately needed more space. If you'd had a cat and wanted to bring it to work, you couldn't have swung it around for fear the poor little thing would bump its bonce on a random stack of boxes, files, or a person.

Brian arranged for me to take a look the next day. As I walked in I was introduced to the current tenant, who was all set to move out at the end of the month. He was an older man, maybe in his sixties, standing about five foot six tall, and by the grumpy look on his face, not happy to have me disturb his day.

But the offices were great, so much bigger than mine. I could imagine myself in them and having room to stretch. So reaching out my hand, I said, 'Hi, I'm Nick Terry.'

There was a reluctance, but he took it and shook. Very odd. Well, no matter.

'Yes, I know who you are,' he said tersely.

Okay, maybe there is a matter.

I tried to smile to break the ice, but the atmosphere was so chilly you'd have been forgiven for nipping off to put on thermals. Yet there was something about this guy. Something more to his story. Almost as though he knew me. And not just by reputation. Something deeper, something more personal. It bugged me that I couldn't put my finger on it.

Putting on my best hey, we're just two regular guys chatting and enjoying the time of day, I asked, 'Have we met before? I'm sure I recognise you.' I didn't, I was pretty sure I'd never laid eyes on him.

'No. Not in person. But you used to work for me.'

'I did?' I was already shaking my head. This was clearly a case of mistaken identity.

Thinking maybe he deserved the full buddy approach, I said, still shaking my head, 'I'm sorry, but I think you must have me mixed up with someone else. I've only ever worked for my dad and a place called Despatch Riders, and as I'm pretty sure you're not my dad...' I smiled. Come on, work with me on this, I thought. 'And DR was owned by Phil and...'

Wait a second. Didn't Phil have a sleeping partner?

The penny dropped.

So that's why he was so cold towards me.

Whoops.

I eventually managed to get a smile from Norman's face, and to be fair, we did over time become friends… well, if not so much friends, we certainly had a mutual appreciation of each other's companies.

About two years later Norman even approached me and asked if I would be interested in selling my company to him. Birmingham Express was growing quickly, and it was my understanding that we had already become bigger than Despatch Riders.

His offer, £10,000, was very tempting. A lot of money for a twenty-year-old. Thankfully, I had a good talking to by Gordon Ketch, who ran a small office supply company from the office along the corridor, and who had become a really good friend, and he advised me not to accept it.

It proved to be great advice.

# Chapter Fifteen

A re you losing weight, son?' Dad asked. We were standing in the kitchen fixing breakfast; which is to say he was fixing breakfast and I was watching him. It was unusual for him to be up this early. In fact, I couldn't remember the last time we were in the same room together.

Was I losing weight? Diane had mentioned it too.

Thing is, work was insane, and, I don't know, maybe because I was still only a teenager I felt I had to prove myself all the time. I was the youngest one on the firm, most of them were married with families. That made a difference. So I packed in the hours. Lots and lots of them. And, well, there wasn't much time for food, and even if there was there were always people milling about, so I couldn't eat even if I wanted to.

Looking down at my trousers, I saw the way they hung from my hips, the belt holding them up on its tightest hole. The shirt above it was tucked in without a hint of a belly beneath it. Then I looked back up at Dad and shrugged. 'I'm off to work,' I said, casual like. 'I'll catch you later.'

The new set of offices were amazing. Gone were the dark and dingy times where you had to pick a route to walk from one end to the other and hope you didn't bash an ankle on the way as you negotiated the clutter of desks and stuff. In its place you could now take a leisurely stroll and even swing your arms if the mood took you, though in reality all I seemed to do was run, but I suppose at least I could now.

Funny to think that all this time the man who worked in here, just a staircase above my previous office, was my old boss. Even funnier to think he knew it and I didn't. What are the odds?

I can't fathom the coincidences in my life. The meaning. Is there even a meaning, or are they just random acts? It's so hard to tell. Whenever I can, I quiz other people about the coincidences in their own lives, but nobody seems to have many. Certainly not to the level of mine.

I often think back to the time when Dad took me back to Yew Tree Cottage the night after he picked me up from school and we ran away together. The thought makes me shudder even now.

When I dwell on it, which thankfully I don't often have time for, but when I do, I wonder if I'm being nudged in the right direction, like there's a path set out for me to take. Pre-destiny is too strong a word, but honestly it's not that far away.

I've wondered if it's a religious thing, but I don't think so. At least it doesn't feel that way.

No, it's something else.

Look, I can't be the first person to think this about someone they love looking down on them, but is my grandad behind it? Yeah, I know there's an element of wishful thinking there, yet it does feel like there's some truth to it too. Is my grandad watching over me and playing a game of chess with my life? Was he manoeuvring pieces on a giant board to ensure things fell into place for me? It did make me wonder. It also made me think that perhaps I should stop being so cautious with my business decisions, maybe start to take more risks and move the company on at a faster pace. After all, if fate was to play a hand in my destiny, then anything I decided could not, within reason, adversely affect my future. Could it? Destiny/the stars/Ouija board/something in the water, call it what you like, Grandad wouldn't let it, would he?

The thought made me think of my grandma. I hadn't been to see her in yonks. Call it a guilt trip, but I decided to nip round and see her after work. She still had the TV I rented to her, but it wasn't owned by me any more. Dad took on that business, though I suspected he never collected any rent from her.

As I pulled up outside her house, I could see a man squinting in my direction. Odd, but okay. Then he started walking towards me. Getting out, I stood by the van.

'Hello,' he said. 'Do you live here?'

'No. I'm just visiting my grandma. She lives at forty-three,' I said, turning and pointing.

'I see. I moved into forty-seven a couple of weeks ago but I haven't met many people yet. I was interested in your van, well not so much the van, but the fact you work for a courier company.'

We both turned to look at the signwriting, at the company name and phone number in big black lettering all down the side.

Admitting I didn't actually work for them but owned it, I said, 'Something you're interested in?'

He nodded. 'I work for Wang Computers, and we've been using taxis to move parts around the country, but they're getting very expensive and, to be honest, not very reliable. It just struck me seeing your van that maybe we should be using a courier. It's just a thought but it makes sense. Any chance you could call in and see me and we can talk it through? Maybe tomorrow?'

And with that he handed me a business card. It read…

*Mr Ernie Sanders*
*Head of Procurement*
*Wang Computers*
*Monaco House*
*Bristol Street*
*Birmingham*

Along with his phone number.

I laughed. 'Gosh, my offices are on Thorp Street. We're less than two minutes away from you.'

I found time the following morning to drop in and see Ernie. I think I was there before he was.

It turned out to be a huge break for me. At the time my turnover was around £1,500 per week. Wang Computers started to spend £500 a week alone.

All because I was thinking of my grandad, and off the back of that I went to visit my grandma. Now look me in the eye and tell me there's not something to the coincidences. I made a mental note to watch out for more, and to always follow where they led. The thought was comforting, like I wasn't alone.

Back to Ernie, whom I discovered did not have a car and caught two buses to work every day and, of course, two buses to get back home. I had another light-bulb moment.

'Hey, Ernie,' I said one day when I called to see him and check he was happy with the service we'd been providing. 'Do you ever take work home with you, maybe a box of files or some other important paperwork?'

'No, not really,' he replied, obviously wondering where I was going with this questioning.

'Oh, that's a shame,' I said, 'because if you had to take some files home every day and then bring them back in the morning, I could provide a van to collect and deliver them for you.'

Still a blank look on Ernie's face.

'And,' I added, 'if you wanted to hitch a ride in the van that would be fine. I can't of course carry you as a paying passenger, for that I would need a licence, like a taxi, and I'm not insured to carry passengers for hire and reward. But I could charge you, let's say a fee of a pound per day, five pounds a week, to take your documents. I could then also offer you a five-pound discount on your weekly invoice in recognition for all the work you're giving us, so in a way, you could argue that the service to and from home, transporting important documents, was for free.'

He still looked blank, but I suspect the idea was starting to sink in. 'You're more than welcome to accompany the package, but I want to be clear, Ernie,' I said, 'we are not,' I emphasised the 'not', 'charging you or providing any sort of taxi service, just a courier service for the movement of documents.'

The biggest smile I had ever seen from his face lit up the room. The penny had at last dropped.

'Nick that would be very helpful, thank you.'

And so it was, every morning and every evening we would send a courier to collect and deliver a small box of highly confidential and very important documents to and from Ernie's house, and amazingly, he always liked to travel with them.

Let's see my competitors try and get this contract off me now.

# Chapter Sixteen

'Fish and chips in the kitchen,' Dad called as I walked in and slammed the door closed behind me, dropping my keys on the hallway table. It had been a nightmare of a day, one thing going wrong after another, and the truth is, you're only ever as good as your last job. Screw it up, even if it's not your fault, and the client will never use you again. That's the harsh reality. Add to that the number of courier firms popping up all over the place – gone are the good old days when there were only a couple of us – and now the clients had a wide choice of who to use, and they knew it. Fortunately we were holding our own, but you had to be on your game every single second of every single day.

There was a mirror on the wall in the hallway right above the table on which I'd tossed my keys. I didn't mean to look into it. And when I did, I didn't mean to stand there staring. God I looked tired. The skin around my eyes sagged, and the bits underneath hung down so low you could have packed your shopping in them.

Shrugging off my suit jacket, I added it to the stack of coats on the bottom of the banister. Tie off next. Then I flicked open the top button on my shirt, revealing skin so white that in the dim hallway light it was hard to tell where the shirt finished and my skin started.

I'd been feeling more and more that there's a compromise you have to make when running a business, that you can either have a strong, healthy company and a clapped-out body, or vice versa. Not both. At least, I couldn't figure out a way to have both.

Taking a deep breath, I turned to go into the lounge, only to come face to face with Dad. I almost banged into him. 'Hey, you startled me,' I said. Had he been standing there watching me?

'I said there's fish and chips in the kitchen for you,' he repeated.

'Yeah, yeah, I know,' I said, brushing it off and making to get past.

He didn't budge. I could smell vinegar on him; the whole place smelled of vinegar.

'So are you going to go and eat it?'

'Maybe later. Can you let me past?'

'No.'

Oh. Stepping back, worried now, I said, 'Okay. I don't understand, what's going on, Dad?'

'I haven't seen you eat anything in months,' he said.

Relief flooded me. 'You had me worried for a moment there!' I exclaimed, laughing.

Not sharing my amusement, he said, 'It's not funny, Nick. I saw you looking at yourself in the mirror there. You've dropped so much weight, and you seriously can't afford to lose any more. You're skin and bone.'

'I'm fine.'

'Well that's the thing, I'm not sure you are.'

I was starting to get irritated now. It had been one heck of a long day and the last thing I needed right now was this.

Losing the smile on my face, I said, 'Can I get past, Dad? I just want to go in and sit down.'

Unmoving, he said, 'But not eat?'

'I might eat later. Look, Dad, fuck's sake, give me a break, okay?'

He grabbed me. We're not a touchy-feely family, and feeling him clutching the upper parts of both my arms felt like an awkward moment between us.

'No, no break. I'm worried about you, son. You're making yourself ill. I want you to go and see the doctor.'

'No way!' But his words had shifted something inside me, as though a nagging voice in the back of my mind that had been droning on and on, to the extent that it had become nothing more than background chatter, had suddenly been isolated and the volume switched up. Hadn't I known something was wrong? Hadn't I just been standing staring at my pasty, knackered, disappearing reflection?

When was the last time I ate? Try as I might, I couldn't remember.

I felt my head sag forward, eyes closing of their own accord. The wave of exhaustion that hit me was epic.

'You can't continue like this,' he said, his voice much softer now.

I nodded, once. It was as much as I could do.

'So you'll go to the doctor?'

Again, I nodded.

'In the morning?'

'In the morning,' I repeated, and I meant it. It was as though I'd been staring at the problem and not seeing it, and now suddenly I could see I was in trouble and had to do something about it. It even felt urgent. If I wasn't so shattered I'd have laughed, so bloody obvious was it now that I'd been screaming at myself to get some help; I just couldn't hear my own voice.

'Good.' He hugged me. We hadn't hugged for years, and it made me feel like a child again, which wasn't unpleasant. Then he turned to leave.

'Dad?'

He turned back.

Smiling, I said, 'Thanks. Oh, one more thing, have I got a doctor?'

His face did the thing faces do when confronted with an unknowable question. 'I've absolutely no idea, son,' he said, and went back into the lounge.

That night I lay on my bed unable to sleep. It's funny how sometimes even exhaustion can't make you drift off. I didn't feel wired, I just felt a huge sense of clarity, as though a fog had lifted. The company was a fair size now. I had fifteen members of staff, all of whom had mortgages and bills to pay and families to keep. The responsibility was a heavy weight to carry, and maybe I hadn't been dealing with it as well as I'd thought.

I guessed the eating thing was stress, but I had absolutely no idea what to do about it. In the morning I'd ring around and find out who my doctor was, then pay them a little visit. But this bout of clarity didn't end there. I knew there was more – Jesus Christ, I felt like one of those snowploughs you see in wintertime, chugging its way through the snow. I could see now just how much I'd been missing on either side of me while I was concentrating on ploughing the company forward.

It took a while of lying there and trying to listen to the voice inside me before realising what the other problem I'd been ignoring was: Diane.

We'd been going out for two years, and the relationship was good, although we didn't see one another anywhere near as much as either of us would have liked. I loved her, and I knew she loved me. But I was working all the hours under the sun… I had to! Often she'd get frustrated when I couldn't see her for days at a stretch, and I didn't blame her. In effect she had a part-time boyfriend, and that was no way to continue. It wasn't healthy.

What she didn't understand, and possibly neither had I until this new sense of clarity had hit, was that although she had a part-time boyfriend, I in turn had a full-time relationship going on behind her back with her as my bit on the side. My full-timer was the company. That was where all my energy, my time, my money and my love, was spent. Speak to any business owner trying to drag their firm to become a success using nothing but blood, sweat and tears, and they'll tell you the level of commitment you need to put in is everything. You give it all, until there's nothing left. The scant scraps of emotion I had left over I'd gladly give to Diane, but that was as much as I could offer her, and it didn't feel nearly enough.

Suddenly I felt really sorry for her.

I knew we were at a crossroads. An intersection. A twoey. Left or right. Left, I could marry her and try and make it work. Or right, we could split up. It's just… I had no idea which way to go.

Finally, exhaustion won the battle and I fell asleep.

In the morning I did my best detective inspector impression and tracked down my doctor. With the appointment booked, I got ready for work and left for the office, via the doctors, leaving Dad looking relieved that I'd kept my promise.

'So, Mr Terry, it's nice to finally meet you,' the doctor said with a grin.

'I don't get ill much,' I said. Should I have felt guilty that I didn't visit him more often?

'Evidently. Now, what's the problem?'

I told him and he nodded. Then he did all the usual tests before declaring, 'There doesn't seem to be any damage yet. But it's only a matter of time. We need to get this sorted. I want you to go and see a psychiatrist.'

Looking up, I said, 'Say that again?'

'I want you to go and see a psychiatrist.'

That's what I thought he'd said. 'A shrink?'

'Not a pleasant term, but yes. As far as I can tell, your problem isn't physical. It's mental. A psychiatrist will help you uncover what's going on and show you how to address it. I'll book you an appointment.'

'Can't you just give me some tablets or something?'

'No.'

'But I'm very busy.'

'I'm sure you are. I'm also sure that's part of the problem.'

'How about I see how it goes?' The thought of going to a shrink scared the bejesus out of me.

'Sure.'

'Really?'

'Yes. And I suggest you pop into a solicitor on the way back to the office and draw up your will. Have you thought about who you'd like to leave your thriving business to?'

'Oh.'

'Shall I book that appointment with the psychiatrist then?'

Hobson's choice. I nodded.

Actually it wasn't as bad as I'd feared. I'm not even sure what I was afraid of, besides the obvious of walking in and them seeing right through me into my soul.

They do have a couch in their office, was my first thought as I walked in. I'd thought that was just a joke, but it's not. I guess I could have laid on it if I'd really wanted to, but I elected for a chair.

'Tea?' he said pleasantly.

'Mm, thank you.' Besides the couch and the chairs, the room was full of books on floor-to-ceiling shelves. 'You read a lot,' I said after he'd got off the phone asking for the brews, which appeared almost instantly.

'Yes, it's part of the job. Now clearly there is some sort of eating disorder going on here. Tell me about your life.'

And so I did. I told him about work and I told him about Diane and home and the sudden bout of clarity I'd had after Dad tackled me over not eating.

'And it's mainly eating in front of other people you struggle with? Don't forget your tea.'

Reaching for the cup, I said, 'Yes. It's like I can't do it. Like it gets stuck in my throat and I have to go and make myself sick. Sometimes I can't remember the last time I ate anything. My Dad's worried about me.'

'I see. Of course, you do realise what you're doing?'

'Reacting to stress?' I offered.

'Oh without question. But I didn't mean that. I meant, you do realise what you're doing right now?'

'Sorry?'

'Your tea. And the biscuit you're eating.'

Looking down, I saw the half-eaten custard cream poking out between my fingers.

Oh stress, Sweet Lady Stress, how you twist and turn and confuse me at every step. As soon as I think I understand you, you go and do this.

In the end I had several sessions with him before he pronounced me fit for purpose, making me promise to go straight back if ever it flared up again.

The relief was incalculable. You know people talk about a weight being lifted from their shoulders? Well, it's true. I felt lighter, more able to deal with life and work. More able to deal with Diane.

I didn't ask her to marry me. It didn't seem fair. No, instead I took the other road: hit the junction and made a sharp right. We split up. Then I dived ever deeper into work.

Initially I'd named the company Birmingham Express so it would come before Despatch Riders in the yellow pages. Now, however, that name felt limiting, as I wanted to expand into other areas. So I did a rebrand, opting for BXT, which stood for Birmingham 'Xpress Transport. While I was at it, I also changed from a sole trader to a limited company.

Ladies and gentlemen, may I introduce you to… drum roll please… BXT Limited.

The evolution of the company also meant I was now buying vans as opposed to renting them, knowing that when they reached two years old I needed to change them for new models. I used a Birmingham auction house to sell them.

One evening, I went from work to watch the vehicles go under the hammer. When I arrived I bumped into the brother of one of my old mates. Martin was a motor dealer and he was there to sell off a few of his own cars. When he asked why I was there, I explained I had a few vans being sold and had come along to watch.

'Oh, you're here to bid on them then?' he said.

'Err, no, I'm here to sell them,' I said.

'No, you need to bid on them yourself to get the price up, all the traders do it.'

'They do?'

'Sure!'

I never knew this and wasn't too sure about the practice. He assured me it was how it worked in the trade, adding that the auctioneer on the rostrum encouraged it because it can help get a bit of momentum going before the hammer comes down.

I had around six vans being sold that night and they all had a reserve on them, which would have been around £2,000 each.

When my first van appeared a few minutes later, I shyly bid on it a couple of times, and once the price had reached £1,800 I ducked out. Sure enough, this policy worked well and the first van sold for around £2,300. I tried my luck again on the second van and everything worked smoothly and the van sold for £2,500 – a good price and well above the reserve.

On the third van, having now got the hang of it, I admit I did get slightly carried away and a tad greedy and I bid as high as £2,000, intending to then stop. There was just silence, no one else bid, and within a few seconds the hammer came down. The auctioneer looked straight at me, pointed at me and shouted, 'Sold!'

Sheepishly I walked up to the rostrum. Without looking down, the auctioneer said, 'Name please.'

Without saying a word, I handed him my business card.

About to copy the details to his form, he paused, looking again at my card, then back to his form. Slowly, switching his gaze to me, he handed back my card, saying, 'Don't ever do that again, Mr Terry.'

I never did.

# Chapter Seventeen

Living with Dad was a mixed bag, part Men Behaving Badly – we weren't always great at housework, probably to be fair because neither of us were there much – and part Timothy Lumsden from Sorry, 'You're how old, and you still live with your dad?' which, in the eighties, applied to anyone over eighteen. So in the rare moments when work wasn't screaming, I'd drive out to areas in which I thought I'd like to live.

I loved these adventures, and would often take long circuitous routes on the off chance I might stumble upon something amazing. But of course, Sod's Law is a rule none of us can avoid, and it was while out working I found something.

I was pulling a late one on a Saturday night, which in the courier game always falls to the boss. It was dark and a bit drizzly so I was driving slowly, trying to peer into the gloom for the correct address to deliver a parcel to. It wasn't really late, maybe ten thirty, but late enough for the boy racers to start fluffing their feathers like some pumped-up turkey and driving like dick-heads. One hit his horn as he whizzed by me, irritated at my slowness, and I wondered, not for the first time, if I wasn't creating a monster with this business that needed unsociable hours to feed it, and the more it grew, the more it demanded.

Oh well, I thought, maybe I'll retire at forty when I'm a millionaire and then I'll drive around the streets in a jazzed-up car, arm out the window, honking my horn. That made me laugh.

It was then I drove past a 'For Sale' sign beside a little end-of-terrace house on a busy main road into Birmingham, called Hagley Road West. This was Quinton, which is the suburb next to Harborne, so I knew it really well. It was less than a mile from my old school.

The following morning I asked Dad if he would come and have a look at it with me. After all, it's a big step buying your first house and felt bigger me being just twenty years old. The house was empty, so we were able to have a look around the plot, peering through all the ground-floor windows.

'Well, what do you think?' I said, standing on the pavement outside.

For the first time I can ever remember, he looked kind of small and kind of lost, and I wasn't sure he knew what to say. Then, steeling himself, he simply said, 'Go for it, son.'

Thinking back, this was the last time I turned to him. I know it's an inescapable part of growing up, the day you realise you've outgrown your parents. But back then, it hit me hard. He had a look I still to this day can't decipher: part pride, part disappointment, with a whole lot of other stuff mixed in.

I looked at him and smiled and nodded, and excited as I was at the prospect of owning my first house, I also felt a heavy weight of emptiness in my belly. I was growing up fast. The business was doing well and I was about to buy my first house. And I understood from this moment, this very second, me and Dad would no longer have the dynamic of father and son. His job was done. From now on, we'd be mates, and that was special in its own way. But it was also different, and we both knew it.

First thing Monday morning I was on the phone to the estate agent and the deal was done.

I moved in and made the little house perfect. I loved it; it was safe, comfy and mine. The mortgage repayments were not too bad, having only paid £19,000 for the property. Looking back at the prices, I wish I'd bought ten and hung onto them all, but of course it's all relative. Even so, for a twenty-year-old, a mortgage of £19k was a huge debt.

Things continued to go well, and my company, albeit still in its infancy, had been trading well and continued to grow. By 1983, still only six years old, I was fortunate enough to enjoy a better income from the business and I thought it was the right time to move home again. After all, I had recently had my house valued and it had doubled in price in just three years.

My office was in the city centre, so home was a direct route down the Hagley Road from Quinton to my offices. Each morning at around 5am, I had to make my way into work diverting around Harborne because I had a little contract with the Queen Elizabeth Hospital.

Every day I collected parcels that needed to be taken to the Royal Mail's central sorting office. In those days it was in Royal Mail Street, Birmingham 1. On my route along Harborne Park Road, I would always look up at a sign that read 'Yew Tree Developments, 24 luxury flats coming soon!'

Obviously the name 'Yew Tree' caught my attention. However, one day the sign changed to read 'Show Home Now Open!'

Yew Tree Developments had built a total of twenty-four flats in two blocks. They were developed by a private builder on the site that was previously a huge old Georgian house. Like all of these historic houses built around that time, it had a very large garden. The house had been pulled down eighteen months before and replaced with twenty-four splendid-looking flats.

I'd kept an eagle eye on the development, and now the show flat was open I decided I should call back later that morning and take a closer look. I liked the idea of owning a flat and not having a garden to maintain. My house in Quinton only had small front and rear gardens, but it took time to tend them, a commodity I did not have. My working week averaged sixty to seventy hours, and often spilled over into more. Taking time out to mow the lawn always felt like I should have been doing something else.

If I was lucky enough to get one of these flats it would mean I was going to be much closer to collect the parcels and post at QE Hospital, so I would get a luxury extra half-hour in bed.

More importantly, I would be back in Harborne where I grew up.

Later that day, I made a trip to view the show flat. I loved it the minute I walked in. Like most builders, the show house had been styled to look fabulous. They had clearly got some clever interior designer to make the most of what was really a fairly small two-bedroom apartment. It was beautifully laid out with some very attractive features, including plaster architrave, ceiling roses and nice dado rails, which was the in-thing in the early eighties.

The show flat was on the first floor, and as you entered from the communal hallway you walked into a small inner hall. On the right-hand side wall was the very latest intercom and camera system to control who was visiting. Visitors would need to press the appropriate button on the panel next to the ground-floor front door and their face would then appear on a little video screen. Very James Bond for its day. On the other side, the developer had fitted a small safe, sunk into the wall, and I immediately had visions of hanging a picture in front of it, an inventive touch I thought. The master bedroom, off to the left, was a good size. This had a compact but beautifully designed en-suite bathroom with a full-size bath, separate shower, sink, toilet and even a bidet for washing your socks in! Well, that's what I was told when I was shown around the flat.

The second bedroom was much smaller but also benefited from an en-suite shower room. The lounge was alluringly presented, with the centrepiece being a marble fireplace on the far wall and two double doors opening onto a small balcony overlooking Harborne Park Road and Grove Park beyond. The kitchen was well fitted out with all major appliances already plumbed in. A small island with two bar stools finished the kitchen layout. Everything a young bachelor could possibly want.

I was smitten. However, the only apartment left for sale was the one I was standing in, the show flat.

Everything else had already been sold off-plan or snapped up by other buyers who were clearly well ahead of the game. The developer who built them, a big chap called Peter, had shown me around the flat himself and told me if he could find any land nearby, he would build another hundred flats and sell them in a day. I believed him.

Peter went on to explain that the only way to secure this last property would be to put down a non-refundable deposit of £1,000 straight away. I think I might have been played, but it didn't matter. I was happy with the price, I adored the flat, I loved the location and I wanted it.

I was determined to get this flat and didn't want anyone else getting their hands on it. Rather than drive back to my office to pick up my cheque book, I arranged for a courier to bring mine out to me. My secretary knew which office desk draw my cheque book was kept in and she thought she could find a good courier company that would deliver it to me. Funny girl!

That was easy, but the hard bit was that although I had recently had my house in Quinton valued, it wasn't even on the market, and I would need the funds from that to put towards my dream flat. I didn't know how I was going to raise a mortgage or if I would even be given one. If I couldn't get a bank or building society to lend me the money, I was going to have to forfeit the deposit of £1,000. In 1983 that was a lot of money to have to write off. Thankfully I knew a man who could help, ironically enough, also called Peter.

My company had done an odd job here and there for Peter James, who was a well-known financial adviser in Birmingham. As soon as I got back to my office I gave him a call and he agreed to meet the following day. He felt sure getting me a mortgage would not be a problem – phew!

The next day Peter, a lovely gentle man, arrived at my office and after a quick coffee together and catch-up on our news, we got down to business. When I told him where the property was he looked up from his notes and smiled. 'You're going to meet my son Kieran then,' he said. 'He's just bought a flat there too.'

What a small world.

Kieran, and his lovely partner Sara and I are all around the same age and became fast friends. Kieran ran his own sports clothing company called Birmingham Race and Rally. Of course, he became a client, using my courier company to deliver sports clothes to various sporting events around the country.

Later Kieran sold his company and qualified to become a financial adviser like his dad, quickly followed by Sara, who did the same. I always liked the way they all worked so well together, I guess it made me think of my dad. So I phoned him.

'Hey, son, good to hear from you, come round,' he said. 'I'll get us fish and chips.'

# Chapter Eighteen

It was 1987, and next year I was going to be twenty-eight. I was getting on, and that kind of maturity brings on a maternal pang. I had it in my head that I wanted a couple of dogs. I thought of Fred often, thought of that morning when I escaped from Mum and Mr Knight and had to say goodbye to him, crouching on the kitchen floor sobbing into his fur and trying to explain why I'd never see him again. That memory still haunts me now, and when I'm tired or stressed and my defences are low, it creeps into my mind with the force of a sucker punch.

That had been twelve years ago, can you believe that? Wow how things had changed.

I'd still not spoken to Mum. She hadn't contacted me, and I'd not picked up the phone to her. I had started to wonder how she was and should I make contact, and if I did, what reaction I'd get. Sometimes I wondered about Peter too, my half-brother.

But you know how these things go. It's one thing wondering and quite another dialling their number. Plus I was manically busy, and that's not an excuse, that's straight up.

However, I knew I couldn't put the day off forever, and when a request came in for a delivery to Amersham, it felt as though the gods were banging me on the bonce with a cricket bat, metaphorically speaking. After making the delivery, I headed towards Mum's address and parked at the top of her street. Do I phone, rock up and knock on the door or drive away? I sat, the engine running, idling as though uncertain what to do next. I thought about Fred, the dog I'd left behind, wondered what became of him. He was about four years old when I last saw him, and given that was some twelve years ago, he'd now be a hundred and twelve in dog years.

Two boys in school uniform walked past the car, slowly, scraping their shoes on the pavement as they walked, bags banging against their legs with each step. Was one of them Peter? He'd be about fourteen now. I wonder what they told him about me?

The longer I sat, the more confused I felt and the more questions bullied my head. I didn't regret what I did, it wasn't that. I guess I just wished I hadn't had to do it, that life had been kinder and I'd felt I'd been able to move in with Dad without all the drama of running away, but at the time there really was no other option.

Yet a part of me missed my mum. That's not easy to write, not easy to admit, but it's true, and sitting here in the car so close to where she lived, the longing to see her felt massive.

How would she react? Would she hug me, or turn her back and flick a dismissive hand in the air? Did she hate me? Did she even think of me? I should go, drive back to the office. This was a stupid idea.

Crossing my arms and sinking back into the seat, I watched the boys, further down the road now. No, Peter would be younger than them, I decided.

It's the not knowing. That's the worst thing. Whatever the situation, however bad, it's the not knowing that makes it worse. Tell me the problem and I can begin to deal with it. Put all of my vast twenty-seven years of maturity behind it. Well, Nick my old son, the problem seems to be you want to see your mum.

Two deep breaths, in out, in out.

Let's go for it. No more thinking, drive to the house and knock on the door.

And that's what I did.

Heart pounding so hard I thought it would pop out of my body, I parked, got out and walked confidently in a kind of 'fake it till you make it' kind of way up the short path to the front door and rang the bell.

Silence, no hundred and twelve-year-old dog barking.

I could hear my breathing, fast and strong. I counted the seconds, and by the time I reached sixty my heart rate had settled back to something akin to normal.

Okay, no one at home, that's good. I've done my bit, made the first move, I'm the winner, I claim the higher ground as my prize. All I have to do now is leave Mum a note and wait for her to call.

As I turned to make my way back to the car for pen and paper, a vehicle slowed and pulled up ahead of me. I didn't need to see inside to know it was them. Gods with cricket bats don't smack you on the head to do something and then leave you high and dry, it's just not their style.

Heart hammering, mouth dry, legs wobbly, I forced my back straight and locked eyes with the person in the passenger seat. Hello Mum.

Was she pleased to see me? Was that a smile developing on her face?

The car stopped just behind mine and Mum was first to get out, Ralph Knight remaining in the driver's seat.

'Hello,' she said.

No fanfare, no rush to hug me, no real emotion. Just 'Hello.'

'Hi,' I said, adding in a tumble of words, 'I was in the area and thought I'd call by,' as though I needed to explain, and I guess justify, why I was outside her house.

'How lovely to see you. Are you stopping long enough for a cup of tea?'

And that was it. The ice was broken and I was invited in as though the last time we had seen each other was only last week, not twelve bloody years ago.

Still, this no-fuss low-key approach worked for me. I'm not sure how I would have coped with lots of emotion, hugs, kisses and more hugs. No, this was very low-key, and it was all I could do to stop myself giving Mum a handshake, something I was doing everyday with my business head on.

Yes, of course there was a part of me that would have loved it had she run up and squeezed the life out of me, but then I have never had that, not even when I was young. No, for me, everything was reserved, as though we were some terribly stuffy family uncomfortable with displays of emotion between ourselves, which I guess we were. Maybe the cuddle strand of our DNA was missing.

I stayed for about an hour and we caught up on news, although I did most of the talking, mainly about my business. She never asked about Dad, and in all the years that I continued to see her she never did, not once, which is funny because Dad would ask after her all the time. Speaks volumes, doesn't it.

Peter was out at friends so I didn't get to see him again this time, but I did get to see him the next time I called around. Soon after this first encounter, she moved back to Gloucestershire to live in a small village called Ruardean. I would continue to see her about twice a year, normally around her birthday and just before Christmas, sometimes meeting in Cheltenham for a coffee. I always loved the time I spent with Mum, especially if she came on her own without Ralph. And although it was always nice to see her, of course it was, it would be wrong to say we were ever really close like a mother and son should be.

She died aged seventy-five in 2007.

I went to her funeral, which was held in the local church, and her ashes were eventually scattered in the nearby Forest of Dean.

Ralph died a couple of years later. I didn't go to his funeral.

As befitting my now maturing age, I'd moved out of the flat and purchased a lovely house in the middle of Handsworth Wood golf course. It sat in the Sandwell Valley, which is a big green belt area separating Birmingham and West Bromwich. The house was half of an old barn that had been converted about thirty years ago. Despite being only four miles from Birmingham city centre, it was like living in the middle of the countryside, and reminded me very much of my time back in Notgrove. Peter and Jackie Stokes lived in the other half of the conversion, which was actually long old milking sheds split into two.

Peter had an office equipment company called Sandwell Office Equipment.

With the house and beautiful garden (yes, I know, but this time I employed a gardener) I decided now was the right time to look at getting some new best canine friends.

I had always wanted a German shepherd because I knew how loyal they were, but I also wanted a golden retriever. Back when I lived in Notgrove, the gamekeeper had a golden retriever and I used to love to watch him round up the pheasants who, rather harshly I thought then, and still do now, were being bred ready for releasing out of the woods for the big shooting day. As a fourteen-year-old I took part in the rite of 'beating', a term used for people who used to walk through the woods beating sticks against the trees to frighten the birds out into flight so the toffs, who had surrounded the woods, could shoot them down. Pheasants, although stunning to look at, are big, slow, ungainly birds, sort of the Mini Metro of the bird world, and are never going to set any speed records, and yet certain people think it clever to take leisurely potshots at them and then call it a sport. I always loved to see the ones that got away, and to be fair a lot of them did; these toffs may have a lot of money, but thankfully they don't have much skill at using double-barrelled shotguns.

One day I was chatting to a friend and mentioned about getting a couple of dogs.

He laughed.

'What?'

'You know I'm a judge at dog shows, right?'

I didn't.

He told me about a breeder friend of his from Crufts who happened to have some all-black, long-haired German shepherd pups for sale. The bonus for me was that the father of the litter had been a champion show dog. No flies on me, that weekend I headed off to Peterborough to meet the puppies and of course the father. He was a huge dog, big body and a very big head. In fact, he looked more like a little black bear. Although he looked fierce, personality-wise he was as gentle as a lamb.

I wanted all the puppies, but in the end I settled on a little shy one in the corner who stole my heart, knowing in that instinctive way you do around animals that we'd be the closest of friends.

'Him,' I said, already picturing us out on walks and hanging out together. 'Can I bagsy him please?'

I was told I could have him when he was nine weeks old. I had a two-week wait before I became a father.

A week later serendipity tapped me on the shoulder when I saw an advert for golden retriever puppies. When I phoned the breeders, who lived in a lovely house in Solihull, they said they had the parents and would be happy for me to meet them when I came to see the puppies, and that made me feel safe buying from them.

Puppies have such a unique smell about them, similar to that of a human baby only with a bit more of a 'poo and wee on wet newspaper' hum about them. I guess you either love it or hate it. Personally, I loved it.

This time I went for the puppy who was the most adventurous and cheeky. Again I was told I would have to wait until the pups were nine weeks old, but this time I was only having to wait a week. So now I was to become the father of two little dogs in a week's time.

The days dragged until finally Saturday arrived. Bright and early – so bright and early I had to park up when I arrived and wait for a civilised time to knock – I set off for Peterborough to collect the German shepherd.

I named him Rebel, after the dog in the TV series Champion the Wonder Horse (who was also a German shepherd, played by canine actor Blaze, who could do amazing tricks). All the way home I talked to him and told him about my life, and how amazing his life was going to be. It just felt perfect and right and we had a connection from the second we were alone together.

The following day I collected the golden retriever. I named him Champion, or Champ for short, for obvious reasons. Same deal, instant connection.

There are always moments in life when you kick yourself for not filming it. When I walked in and was met by Rebel, who had been left on his own for two hours while I had gone to collect his brother, I knew I'd missed recording one of the most gorgeous moments of my life. The two of them sniffed and played and tumbled about like the cutest double act you've ever seen.

'Oh! My! God! They are adorable!' Jackie exclaimed. She and Peter had nipped in from next door knowing my babies had arrived. There's a grin reserved for puppies that's unlike any other, and it was all over their faces.

And mine.

Keen to set the routine, when Peter popped his head around the door that Friday night and shouted, 'Pint?' I readily agreed.

'Oh,' he added, sheepishly moving to one side to reveal Jackie hiding behind him, 'and I come with a babysitter, if that's okay?'

Our local was called The Vine, found on the corner of a street of terrace houses about two miles from where we lived. It was your basic traditional pub full of locals and selling great locally brewed beer… think the Rovers Return on TV's Coronation Street. But The Vine had one big difference. This was run by a lovely Indian family who provided the best chicken curry to be found anywhere in the West Midlands.

Peter and I would try to make it most Fridays, and we would often be joined by two Tonys. Tony Lister, who ran a very successful and established family business called James Lister & Sons, based in West Bromwich – his company was best known for engineering supplies and services and it was first established in 1874. It would be fair to say that Tony Lister had been there, seen it, done it and had the T-shirt to prove it.

The other Tony was Tony Baggott, a very successful lawyer working in Birmingham for the company Putsman & Sons.

We would spend many a Friday night after a hard week at work sharing stories over a pint and a curry on what sort of week we had endured, the four of us trading tales that got ever more embellished the more we drank. It was our form of therapy at a time when that didn't really exist. A way of talking it out in an attempt to stay sane. Although we all had different backgrounds and ran different companies, there was always a familiar theme running through our various stories.

It must have been some six months after I had first got my dogs that during our usual Friday night Vine club meeting, as we had called ourselves, Peter asked me, 'When was the last time you went on holiday, Nick?'

'Blimey, now there's a question. Nope, can't remember.'

Then he said something that made my heart sing. 'You know, if you ever wanted to, we'd look after the dogs.'

Only a fool would ignore such a kind offer. He must have seen the cogs spinning, and laughingly said, 'Where would you go?'

Now that was easy. The one place I'd always wanted to see. 'Florida.'

Never one to hang about if a thought felt good, I did as much as I could to ensure everyone at work was briefed on what to do, and more importantly what not to do, and I departed from Heathrow airport for my well-earned break in Florida.

It was a long way to go for a week, but that was as long as I felt I could justify being away from the business.

I'd decided on a villa. Hotels always feel restrictive somehow, and besides, it had its own private swimming pool. The place was exactly as I'd hoped, luxurious and spacious with four bedrooms, a nice big lounge and open-plan kitchen. The pool was at the back and thankfully covered in black see-through netting to keep those pesky midges from biting. It had the usual immaculate garden to the front and, like all the properties there, a double garage that housed the biggest washing machine and dryer I had ever seen. More like the commercial machines you see in laundrettes than those we have back home. For a while I stood staring at it, wondering who comes on holiday intent on industrial levels of cleaning.

The villa was in the tranquil neighbourhood of Davenport, about a twenty-minute drive to all the main attractions in Florida, including Sea World, Universal Studios and of course Disney World.

On the first morning I hired a car, just a little zip-about, and set off to get a feel for the place and pick up some basic provisions, and for basic provisions read beer. As someone who makes their livelihood from vehicles on the road, I can't describe how odd it felt getting in the wrong side of the car and driving out onto the wrong side of the road. What's even more odd is how I couldn't stop grinning as I did it. Little things, I guess.

Having found a supermarket and bought everything I felt I needed to kick back and enjoy my time there (yep, read beer again), I spotted a carousel of postcards, all with the stamps pre-attached! Such a simple idea, but when you're somewhere strange trying to figure out where everything you need is, it felt like magic. America's like that; it's a smart country to visit. Anyway, I picked one intending to send it to Peter and Jackie back home, to let them know I had arrived safely, that the villa was lovely and that I hoped that the dogs were both okay.

Of course, I then did what we all do in similar circumstances, wrote it and popped it on the dash of the car, where it sat for the next couple of days. The trouble was, try as I might, I couldn't find a postbox anywhere. If I didn't see one soon, I would be back home in the UK before the postcard.

With the postcard still on the dashboard on day three, and getting a bit desperate now, I decided to act. I'd seen a tourist information centre just a few blocks down (there you see, I'd even started speaking the language), so I made a point of heading that way next time I was out.

The car park was huge; they don't do things by halves over there. I parked up and made my way over, opening the door and receiving the standard blast of air conditioning that hits you like a cool bath of air. Honestly, it's worth going shopping just for that.

A middle-aged lady sat behind the counter, and clutching my postcard I went up and asked, 'Have you any idea where I can find a postbox to post this, please?'

Her reply was a real education, and even today I still think it's a brilliant idea and wonder why we have not adopted the same system here in the UK. We do tend to copy everything the Americans do – eventually!

First, she suggested that I hand it in at the reception of the hotel I was staying at. Once I told her that I was staying in a villa, she said, 'Have you noticed a postbox at the end of your drive, probably on top of a tall wooden post?'

'Yes, but isn't that for delivered post to the house?'

'Well yes,' she said, and went on to explain the American system. On the side of the box is a flag in the down position, and she advised I raise it and place my postcard in the box. The postman would see the flag on his rounds and know immediately to collect any outgoing post that had been left.

'Wow,' I said, laughing. 'What a great idea. I'll do that tonight when I get back.'

Smiling, she offered to take the postcard from me and add it to their own pile of post that had still not been collected that day.

Handing it over, I said, 'That's so kind, thank you.'

'It's no trouble.'

For the first time I recognised her English accent. Keen to be friendly as she'd been so helpful, I said, 'Whereabouts in the UK are you from?'

'Oh, a place just outside Birmingham.'

'Really? Where?'

'How well do you know Birmingham? It's a place called Sandwell.'

My face must have done the 'are you for real?' look. 'I live in the middle of Sandwell Valley. What a small world,' I said, shaking my head.

'Ha! Isn't it? I used to work for a company called Sandwell Office Equipment.'

Okay, now the shivers on the back of my neck were starting.

'The one run by Peter Stokes?'

Leaning forwards, her face a half-grin, half-shock, she said, 'You know him?'

Oh I can go one better than that. Lady, hold onto your hat. 'You are not going to believe this. Take a look at the postcard,' and I nodded at it still in her hand.

I could see the gooseskin erupt on her forearms as she peered at the name and address. 'Oh. My. God,' she whispered.

My sentiments exactly.

Of all the gin joints, in all the towns, in all the world…

When her shock subsided, she asked, 'Can I write a note on it?'

She did. I wish I could have seen Peter's face when he read a postcard from his next-door neighbour and his old PA sent from Florida.

Once I had returned to the UK I couldn't wait to pick up the phone and call Dad to tell him. Like me, he also often had strange coincidences happen to him, and we would regularly phone each other to relay our various stories.

When I called him to tell him my latest coincidences, he said, 'Son, you should write a book about all these.'

Now there's a coincidence. I have now!

One for the book.

# Chapter Nineteen

If you're American, you'll know all about Thomas Jefferson. He was a Founding Father, and there are a lot of quotes attributed to him, but my favourite has always been: 'I'm a great believer in luck, and I find the harder I work, the more I have of it.' Oh boy, isn't that the truth.

By 1996 things were going well. The business was growing month on month, which of course is a double-edged sword because that required increasing amounts of me, and there wasn't a heck of a lot left to give. In terms of hours put in, I could have sat down with a bunch of junior doctors and held my own. But I was always open to new opportunities, because... well, that's business.

That was when I secured a new contract with Severn Trent Laboratories.

Initially, it just involved a number of drivers going around to various collection points to pick up samples of bottled water. These samples were controlled by STW's own technicians. The vast majority of these collections were from petrol stations. All garages are given a small tolerance of how much spilt petrol and diesel can be splashed onto the forecourt floor and washed into drains when drivers are filling up their cars.

When you drive into garages you often drive over a small metal grid that runs the length of the forecourt entrance. These drains collect the oil and water from the sloping forecourts and from these drains the water samples are taken. Each sample is placed in a small glass bottle, and we got the contract to collect the bottles and deliver them to the STW testing labs based in Coventry.

Each bottle would then be analysed to ensure the percentage of oil was within the limits allowed.

Part of the deal was that I'd have regular meetings with Rachel Gurney, the managing director of Severn Trent Labs to discuss how the contract had been going. The meetings were productive and pleasant, and she was always nice to deal with.

Her office was immaculate, her desk pristine. I often wondered how someone so busy could be so tidy. Sipping coffee, we went through the pleasantries and both agreed the contract was running just fine.

'Out of interest,' I remarked, 'how difficult is it to take the samples?'

'It's not.'

Cogs in brain started spinning like Formula One wheels on a hot lap. 'Really?'

And that's what I mean about luck.

A few weeks later, after giving a team of my drivers some training, particularly on health and safety, the contract was rewritten to include taking the samples and then delivering them to the labs. This meant an increase in our charges, worded as 'added value services'. The couriers all got paid extra and Severn Trent redistributed their manpower.

The increase in our charges doubled overnight, yet the extra costs to me were very limited.

Profit margin increased: tick.

Customer happy: tick.

Drivers delighted: tick.

A win-win situation.

I couldn't help thinking it was time for a treat.

Holidays were as scarce as hen's teeth, yet sometimes you've got to take the opportunity or you'd never get away. I went to Florida last time, where else did I fancy? I know, how about Egypt?

I was still living at the same house on Handsworth golf course with my two boys, Rebel and Champ. Up until this point, whenever I needed a dog-sitter, my neighbours Peter and Jackie were on hand, but it turned out on this occasion they were booked to be away at the same time.

Not to be deterred, I made some phone calls and came up with a pretty good plan B when a couple of friends jumped at the chance to move in and take care of the boys.

Irene and her partner were old friends. I'd known her since she had a Saturday job in the hairdressers a few doors down from where I grew up in Harborne. Now she was working for the Crown Prosecution Service in Birmingham. It was a job-share situation for her.

'The only thing is, Nick, I'm full-time next week. The girl I share with is also away, seems it's a popular time for it.'

'That's fine,' I said. I'd converted the garage into a doggy day-care den, like a canine man cave, with sumptuous sofas and rugs and a radio switched to Radio Four to keep them entertained. They even had a flap to the outside so they could pop in and out as they pleased.

Fiona and Tom were both big dog lovers and had met my two on numerous occasions. I knew they were really looking forward to staying at my house, looking after dogs and taking them on long walks around the Sandwell Valley.

Happy, I flew to Egypt, staying in the Sheraton Hotel in Luxor on the banks of the River Nile. It was certainly a fascinating place to visit. You really get a sense of age and history, and the area known as the Valley of the Kings blows you away, but so does the poverty on the streets. That was hard to see and really affected me.

While I was there I booked into every excursion a visitor was expected to see. Lots of us did, and I'd see the same smiling faces on the coaches or queuing in line, and we'd do the British thing of nodding and grinning.

Many of the people were older, but there was another couple around my age I constantly nodded to.

I first saw them when I was in line to check in at the hotel. I didn't think anything about it, but the next morning at breakfast they were sat at the table next to me. Later that day, having ventured over to the Valley of the Kings, I saw them again coming out of the 'Tomb of Ay' just as I was going in. By this stage, they had clearly clocked me too.

It became a bit of a joke; every time I ventured out, there they were.

The week shot by, and before I knew it, there I was in line to check out at the hotel reception desk. Guess who was in front of me? Yep, the couple.

On the coach to the airport, they were next to me again.

And standing to board the aircraft and doing what the British do so well, queuing in a neat tidy line, I turned to them and said, 'I keep seeing you everywhere I go, are you following me?' They laughed and admitted that they too had noticed me time and time again.

Clearly, with a week of inadvertently spending so much time together, it felt acceptable to introduce ourselves – oh, how British we are!

'Lin and John,' they said.

'Nick,' I replied.

The plane must have been delayed, because we were there for some considerable time, and after the holiday talk had been exhausted, conversation turned to home.

'So where do you live?' Clearly, as we were all standing in a line to catch the flight back to BHX airport, there was a reasonable chance that they lived in or at least close to Birmingham, and it transpired they did. We knew the same pubs, restaurants and clubs, and then something came up about having time off work and how difficult that can be.

'I work for myself,' I said, 'and you would think getting time off would be easy, but it was a nightmare.'

'I know!' Lin said, looking animated. 'You want to try working for the Crown Prosecution Service.'

You know in the Tom and Jerry cartoons when Tom does a double take? Yep, that was me.

'In Birmingham?'

Nodding, she said, 'Yes.'

'No way. My friend works for the CPS in Birmingham, maybe you know her, Irene?'

Her turn to do a cartoon double take.

'You know Irene?'

'Know her,' I said, laughing. 'She's currently in my house looking after my dogs.'

'Oh my God, you're Nick! I job-share with Irene. Before we came away we were on the phone constantly talking about how much she was looking forward to staying at your house!'

Mental note, phone Dad and tell him as soon as we land. I knew what he'd say: 'One for the book, son.'

Okay, okay, okay, guess who was sitting next to me on the plane? I've no idea, but they were close by, close enough for me to reach across and invite them to a party I was throwing in a couple of weeks' time.

'Irene's going to be there. Don't say anything to her, it'll be such a laugh to see her face when you walk in!'

Two weeks later, with the party in full swing, I heard the front doorbell go, and although I couldn't see from where I was standing in the kitchen, I knew Lin and John had just arrived because I could hear loud shrieks and laughter and then someone shouting, 'I didn't know you would be here!'

The odd thing was, it wasn't Irene, who was standing right next to me in the kitchen. It turned out another of my long-standing friends also knew Lin.

And the world just gets smaller, and smaller, and smaller.

'Dad, another one for the book?'

# Chapter Twenty

I soon felt the company had reached its potential in Birmingham. We were well established and had the lion's share of the business in the area. Sure it was an ongoing daily battle to maintain that position, but we had a good reputation and a brilliant team.

So, where next?

I had options, such as London, which I quickly discounted, as anyone with a clapped-out moped was setting themselves up as The City's Premier Courier Company! And while I'm all for competition, the thought of being undercut by Dave on his Vespa was too depressing.

But I did open offices in Coventry, Warrington, Newmarket, Cambridge, Bristol and Nottingham.

Although my base was always in Birmingham, I'd drive out for meetings. I didn't mind the commute; I had a lovely new Range Rover that glided through the miles.

Our Cambridge branch had just secured a really cool contract and I drove up for a Thursday evening meeting. In attendance were the branch manager, his assistant, and a team of twelve drivers who were all due to start on Monday morning to work on the new contract, which was with Addenbrooke's Hospital.

The contract required us to collect blood samples from various doctors' surgeries in and around Cambridgeshire that needed delivering as soon as possible to the pathology lab at Addenbrooke's, ensuring the samples remained in good condition. Each and every blood sample needed to be stored in fridges within the surgeries and then once collected would be transported by us in cool boxes. We had also won the contract to provide a minibus service from Tesco's car park to Addenbrooke's, but the only passengers allowed were Addenbrooke's nursing staff. Like most hospitals, parking was a nightmare on-site, so the hospital had agreed to rent some parking spaces from the nearby Tesco store and we provided courtesy transport for the nurses back and forth throughout the day.

Around six thirty, the office phone rang, which was unusual at that time of the evening. Normally, all after-hours calls would get diverted straight to the head office in Birmingham, where the switchboard was open twenty-four seven. The branch manager Margaret broke away from the meeting and took the call.

'Nick,' she said, walking back in, 'it's your brother. He's asked to speak to you urgently.'

Paul? God, I hadn't spoken to him in decades. I left the room and made my way over to the phone.

In the twenty steps it took to go from the meeting to the phone, an entire movie of memories, images and emotions whizzed through my mind. Me and Paul as kids were never very close, but seeing as we shared a room, we were constantly around one another. Then of course the bickering and arguing, as boys do, and on occasion the fighting, which, as he was older and bigger, he always won unless I could run away before he clouted me.

Paul was always Mum's favourite, a fact she never hid. He was very bright academically, easily passing his eleven-plus, going to a top grammar school and then straight after school attending the Britannia Royal Naval College at Dartmouth. At just twenty-one years old he became one of the youngest officers to reach the position of lieutenant. After leaving the navy a couple of years later, he became an inspector for the Hong Kong Police.

Was he phoning me from Hong Kong, or was he back in the UK now?

When was the last time I'd spoken to him?

I knew the last time I'd seen him. That was easy, it was the day the family left Notgrove for Amersham in 1975. He stayed with a friend so he could complete his school exams.

Now he'd tracked me down to Cambridge. For a second I wondered how he did it, but he was a police inspector, it would have been child's play for him to get the number from my Birmingham office. But it would have taken effort. Which meant this wasn't a 'hey bruv, long time no see' catch-up call.

'Hi stranger,' I said, lifting the receiver from the desk. 'To what do I owe the pleasure?'

'I have some bad news. I have cancer and it's spread all over my body, and I'm not sure I am going to be around much longer. I need to tell Dad, and you know what he's like, he gets so emotional, so I was hoping you could be there when I tell him?'

Wooo!

No Hey Nick, how are you? What's life like? Is the weather good over there? Just, bang! I've got cancer. I'm dying. The sheer directness made my head spin.

So many questions.

Jesus!

'Nick?'

Pulling myself together, I said, 'Yes, of course I'll be there.'

Once the initial shock had passed, I asked him what had happened? How did he know? Why can't he get treatment? I suppose all the usual questions that spring to anyone's mind when they hear such news.

Paul explained that about a year ago he had become aware of a small lump in one of his testicles, so went to see his local doctor. She was a young and rather inexperienced doctor and had simply told Paul it was just a cyst and not to worry about it. It wasn't, it was cancerous, and if it had been diagnosed correctly it could have been removed, and the chances were all would have been fine.

Testicular cancer happens to be one of those cancers that if caught early there is a very good chance of making a full recovery. Unfortunately for Paul, due to getting the wrong diagnosis over the last year, his cancer had spread. He realised something was seriously wrong when he first felt a small lump on his neck. This small lump had now become the size of a tennis ball.

My head was everywhere. I couldn't think straight. Part of me was concentrating on Paul, but it was like another part of me had spun off to remind me about something that I knew had been jumping up and down in my head for attention for months.

This thought had been bugging me. Bugging and bugging and bugging me. But I'd ignored it. Shushed it. Pushed it away.

Now, it was like a theatre sign on Broadway: big and bold and unmissable.

And it said: you have a lump on your testicle too!

I'd found it a few months earlier. And ignored it. I was too busy to be ill. It would go away. Just ignore it and it'll go away.

Dad always said things happen in twos. And it's true, they do. Something would happen to me and I'd tell Dad and he'd say, 'You're not going to believe this, but...'

Even when we were kids, things that happened to me would happen to Paul, and vice versa.

It was a family trait.

Oh God no.

The meeting was brought to an abrupt end, and although I had a hotel room waiting for me in Cambridge, I chose to drive straight home that night.

At eight thirty the following morning I was standing in my doctor's reception, insisting that even though I didn't have an appointment, I had to see a doctor. The receptionist could see I was in severe distress and told me to take a seat and she would somehow fit me in.

Driving back the previous night, I had cried most of the way; God only knows how I managed to drive safely. My head was bombarding me with thoughts of Paul and all the emotions surrounding that, but also the fact that I must have cancer too.

I felt sick and I felt scared and I felt sad and I felt guilty for everything I was feeling, as though they were all the wrong ones, but I didn't know what the right ones were! I couldn't think straight no matter how hard I tried. I was dying. We both were. Me and Paul.

All I kept hearing in my head was Dad saying, 'Things come in twos, son.'

Thankfully it turned out to be a cyst, although after getting it checked, I did then go and get a second opinion. I certainly wasn't going to take any risks that they had got my diagnosis wrong.

Paul had decided to fly back from Hong Kong to tell Dad the news, and we did that a couple of nights after his phone call. It was awful, one of the hardest things I've ever had to do.

He also wanted to trace Mum to tell her. For that, he was on his own.

God bless the NHS. He got specialist treatment at the Gloucester Royal Hospital where they cut away the lump in his neck and put him on a course of chemo to fight the cancer that had spread throughout his body.

Initially, this treatment was thought to have been successful, but then about six months afterwards the cancer had spread to his brain and he was taken to the Royal London Hospital for further treatment. I went to visit him the night before his operation. Paul explained they were going to cut into the top of his head, while he was still awake, to see if they could remove the lump that had grown there. It was a delicate operation. He needed to remain conscious throughout so the surgeons could constantly talk to him while they operated.

Paul didn't want to, or couldn't sleep, so I spent the evening by his bedside and we just talked endlessly. We covered all sorts of topics, even going back to the day when I had first heard Mum and Dad arguing from the bottom of the stairs.

Giving me a sideways look from his bed, he said, 'I wasn't a brilliant brother, was I?'

Laughing, I said, 'No, you were a bastard!'

Grinning ear to ear, he said, 'I know I was. I'm sorry.'

I shook my head, fighting back the tears. 'No need.'

My overall memory of that night was how brave Paul was, and he assured me he had no fear of dying. He explained he'd had a great life, experienced so many things, including being a passenger in a fighter jet while taking off and landing on the Ark Royal, a Royal Navy aircraft carrier. He said it was just one of the many highlights in his life.

Thankfully the operation went really well, and a couple of months later he was able to return to Hong Kong, telling everyone he was fine and the cancer had gone.

He collapsed and died a few months later while playing golf on his favourite course. I think he knew all along he was not going to live. It was 9th April 1995. He was just thirty-seven years old.

I flew out to Hong Kong to attend his funeral, the only family member to go, which speaks volumes about my parents. It was a very moving service held at the Union Church, Wan Chai in Hong Kong. The police laid on a spectacular service.

Paul was given a full military service send-off, and I was okay and holding myself in check until a single officer from the Hong Kong Police played the last post, and I lost it, sobbing for the brother that in his final months had become my friend.

Paul's best friend, Sean, stood by me and helped me get through the service.

I stayed on in Hong Kong for a few days before flying back with Paul's ashes. The memorial was held a few weeks later at St Peter's Church in Winchcombe, Gloucestershire.

It was wonderful to see so many of his friends and our uncles, aunts and cousins. It's just a shame it was under such sad circumstances.

Mum and Ralph were there, but Dad refused to go because Mum was going. Honestly, I'm lost for words sometimes.

After the funeral, probably because of the funeral, I decided to make some changes in my life. Major changes.

# Chapter Twenty-one

Change can either be something you effect, or something you except. The business changes I made after Paul's death were all things I effected, purposely setting out to make alterations that might make running the company smoother. But in my personal life, it was more a case of opening myself up to opportunities and learning to accept them.

The first one happened back in the doctor's waiting room. I'd been out of my mind with worry since Paul had told me about his diagnosis, convinced I had the same, and had parked myself in the waiting room determined not to move until a doctor had seen me.

It was a long wait.

Desperate for anything to draw my attention away from my impending demise, I picked up a copy of the Daily Mail that someone had left behind. Flicking through, more just looking at pictures than anything else as I couldn't really focus on the stories, I spotted a headline that did make me go 'Oh!' It read:

Lovell Construction Española
Elviria, Marbella
NOW OPEN!
Weekend inspection trips available
With free hire car

Lovell Construction rang a bell. A loud one. They were clients with offices a few miles north of Birmingham.

The article went on to say that Lovell Española, a subsidiary of Lovell Construction UK, were nearing completion on the first wave of homes at their thirty-million-pound White Pearl Beach development near Marbella.

Lovell was building a total of 120 homes and were inviting potential buyers over to view them for the bargain price of a hundred and fifty quid.

Included in that price were return flights from Birmingham to Malaga Airport, three nights in one of the finished apartments at White Pearl, and a free rental car to use during your stay to explore the area. They even said arrangements would be made to meet you at Malaga Airport and drive you to the development. I do love a bargain!

I decided that if I didn't have cancer, I was going to book myself on one of the trips, and after the all-clear, that's what I did. The thought process was that I needed a bolthole, a safe haven, a work-free/stress-free zone.

Funny how the threat of cancer makes you appreciate life.

About a week before I was due to fly out, a small package arrived containing my flight tickets, some information on where to go when I landed at Malaga Airport, and a videotape.

The tape was a short but stylish promotional film about White Pearl Beach, which only increased my excitement. I noticed at the end of the film that it went on to play a short feature about another development that Lovell had been involved in but was now fully sold called Puebla Aida. This was slightly further along the coast back towards Fuengirola. I made a mental note to take a look at this, as I thought it might give me a good idea of the quality of the finish of Lovell's work.

Lovell organised these inspection visits extremely well. I had prepared myself for a hard sell when I arrived but nothing was further from the truth. As promised, I was met at the airport in Malaga on Saturday morning and then there was a twenty-minute ride to the White Pearl Beach development in Elviria, about five miles short of Marbella. I was given a key to my apartment, which was mine for the next two nights, and a key to a rental car. I was told if I needed anything to just pop back to reception, which was also the sales office, and they would be happy to help. I was told there was a show flat open between ten and six every day, and to feel free to wander in and take a look.

After unpacking, I went to look at the show apartment. I'm always impressed by what a good job interior designers can do on show properties, and this was no exception. I even met the designer, who said, 'Sorry, last-minute titivating,' as she plumped cushions and straightened already perfect curtains.

I said, 'It looks amazing,' and it did.

She seemed pleased and spent a few minutes explaining what she had done and why she had chosen the furnishings, colours and fabrics she had, while I nodded and pretended I knew what she was talking about.

I loved her enthusiasm and her passion. She was so friendly and open and blonde and Swedish and pretty, and did I mention she was blonde? And pretty?

Part of me wondered if I should ask her out, but I'd just landed and it felt a bit predatorial to do so in a business environment. Besides, there was no way she was going to be single.

'Can I tell you something in confidence?' she asked.

'Anything.'

'The last buyer negotiated a free interior design service included in the price.'

Interesting.

'I'm Elona, by the way.'

'Nick Terry,' I said, way too formally. 'Sorry, force of habit. Um, I'm Nick.'

'If you need anything, just ask for me. Okay?'

Smiling, I assured her I would.

Throughout the weekend I was shown various apartments, and the ones I liked were on the front of the development overlooking the sea. They had a clear view of the beach beyond a small piece of scrubland that lay between the two.

'That scrubland can never be built on,' they said.

Mmmm.

But, of course, these apartments were more pricey. 'Because of the view, you understand.'

I needed to think.

The following day, late Sunday afternoon, I decided to go and find Puebla Aida, the other development that Lovell's had finished building a couple of years previously. It was relatively easy to find, about two miles inland from Fuengirola, and you had to drive through Mijas golf course to get to it.

I was struck by the beauty of this place, like no other new development I had seen before.

Puebla Aida was first dreamt up by a Spanish architect who took his inspiration from historic villages dotted around southern Spain. Although this was a new development, you would think you had stepped back in time and were standing in a traditional old Spanish village.

The houses were higgledy-piggledy in their layout, yet I imagine they were meticulously planned to provide an idyllic village setting. You could see that old clay roof tiles had been used, along with stained timber, wrought-iron railing, and fences. There were small swimming pools dotted around, pots, fountains and mini streams. All of this was complemented by beautifully laid out gardens. It was, and still is to this day, a magical place.

Sadly, the architect who had started the development got into financial trouble when he had only just finished phase one, and was unable to complete the project. Lovell Española bought it from him together with the rights to finish phases two and three. Thankfully, and in my view very sensibly, Lovell kept the build in line with the original concept and design.

Standing at the top of the complex, leaning on a wrought-iron fence enjoying the views over the golf course and the town of Fuengirola beyond, it felt magical. The sun had just started to set. It was a warm evening, the place was still and very quiet, apart from the noise of the birds making their way home to nest. For the first time in I don't know how long, I felt my body relax.

A lady came out of a small apartment and stood close by to enjoy the last rays of sunshine.

'Beautiful isn't it,' I said.

'It sure is,' she replied.

'Do you live here?'

'No, I'm staying with my sister Josie. She lives here permanently now.'

'Gosh, how lucky. I would love to own one, but I assume they're all sold?'

'Well, that penthouse has just come on the market as a resale,' my new friend said.

Turning around, I looked up at a pretty three-storey building and for the first time noticed a small 'For Sale' sign hanging off the balcony rails.

That's got my name on it, I thought.

First thing Monday morning, I called the agent, who said he was only too delighted to show me the penthouse.

It was much smaller than the apartment I was staying in at White Pearl, but it didn't matter, I was in love. It was rustic and had fantastic views. Added bonus was, it was a third of the price of the White Pearl Beach apartments I had been looking at.

This was my last full day in Spain. I was due to be taken back to the airport the next day so I couldn't waste any time. I offered the full asking price if they included all the furniture. The agent made a call to the owner, and I was told if I paid a ten per cent deposit it was mine.

'Do you take debit cards?'

'Yes,' the agent said. 'If you'd like to follow me back to my office we'll sort out the contracts.'

In Spain, once the deposit is paid, that's it. The property is taken off the market and you never get into a bidding war, or what is known as gazumping. The only downside is, if you don't proceed you lose your deposit.

The deal was done, the agents even recommended a good lawyer, and within a couple of months I returned to Spain to collect the keys.

I wasn't overkeen on the furniture that came with it, and I'd noticed a large furniture store called A. Benitez not too far away, and decided to drop in.

It was a large impressive shop with far too much choice. The first person I saw was Elona, the interior designer I had met at White Pearl Beach a couple of months earlier. She worked here and remembered me from White Pearl. We chatted and she agreed to give me a quote for a full interior design package, including all furnishings, fittings, and decoration. How perfect!

Three days later, just before I was due to fly back to Birmingham, I handed Elona a set of keys and she promised that by the time I returned it would be finished – and it was. This was now my secret getaway whenever work allowed, and it became something of a lifeline.

It was perfect, and it's down to you, Paul. It's down to you, brother.

# Chapter Twenty-two

'Things come in twos, son.' Dad's words rattled around my brain, and try as I might, I couldn't shake them, because in our family, that's how things are. If one of us has a prang in our car, chances are someone else will have car trouble. If one of us is ill, someone else will be too. Or good… it happens with good things too. Once, Dad and I both won on the scratch cards, both the same amount, on the same day, and neither of us knew the other one was doing it. And that's the other part of 'Things come in twos, son.' How it always seems to be an equal amount, like it has to balance somehow. What happens to one will happen to the other with the same value. It's really odd.

We'd lost Paul and I'd had the cancer scare, so I did what anyone would do in the circumstances and made changes to my life. Spain was a big part of that. I felt like I now had somewhere I could disappear to when things got too much, just for a day or two. But the very fact that I needed it felt like a warning that the business was becoming too much for one person to handle.

'Things come in twos, son.'

I was trying to eat healthily; I think I'm always going to struggle with that, but it wasn't getting on top of me the way it once had. I also had my boys, Rebel and Champ, so I was getting plenty of exercise.

'Things come in twos, son.'

I was doing all the things I could practically do to keep myself in good condition.

'Things come in twos, son.'

So why did it feel like it wasn't enough?

'Things come in twos, son.'

The business. I had to make changes to the business. And I had to do it now.

But while that's a fact, I stopped worrying that things come in twos. Because they did, and it happened. Only, it wasn't me it happened to. It was Peter, my half-brother.

The last time I'd seen him he was a baby who cried all the time. Apparently, he'd grown up and got married. Then the family curse hit – 'things happen in twos, son' – and for one death, there had to be another.

His young wife, Michelle, was killed in a car accident. She was the only passenger and the only one to suffer. The two drivers, both lads, young, reckless and both high on drugs, walked away from the accident with no more than a few scratches. Neither driver in this head-on crash had any insurance.

Peter and Michelle had a four-year-old daughter, but thankfully she wasn't in the car.

I can't imagine what that must have been like for him. After that, he didn't just fall off the rails, he took a neutron bomb and blew them to smithereens. He was angry and got in with the wrong crowd and ended up doing time in prison. The sentence was harsh, ten years I believe.

Two deaths in the family.

Makes you think.

I knew the company was too big for one person to control, yet I'd been hanging onto it with my fingertips because the thought of handing over some of the responsibility to anyone else was terrifying. BXT was my baby and nobody knew it like me. Or had so much invested.

But I was at a crossroads. I could turn left and continue as I was, risk burnout, illness or worse, or I could turn right and move the business from entrepreneurial to a fully fledged managed company.

Everything screamed turn right. I knew it was the correct decision, but when you've been doing something one way for so long, it's really hard to change it no matter how obvious.

Most of my clients now had firm contracts in place and required regular collections and deliveries. I had also moved into a more specialised courier side of the business and had contracts with the likes of Severn Trent Water, North West Water, Siemens Computers, Blockbuster Video, Digital Equipment Company, Good Hope Hospital and Addenbrooke's Hospital.

In fact, over ninety per cent of the work BXT undertook now was for blue-chip companies. Over the previous ten years, I hadn't had a single bad debt to write off. Some of these large companies could be a little slow in paying but I was always confident I would get paid in the end.

Blockbuster Video was a great contract. We were tasked with taking care of their point of sale hardware: tills, barcoding scanners and printers. If any Blockbuster shop had a problem with any of their equipment, anywhere in the UK (they had around 200 video stores in their heyday) we would collect a replacement part from the nearest store warehouse we controlled, arrive on-site, swap out the faulty equipment and return the broken part back to our central branch in Birmingham, where we had our own in-house repair centre. Once the part had been fixed it would be returned back to the store it came from ready to go back out if needed. We were much more than a courier service and that was also our strapline: 'BXT – more than a courier service.'

My dinner party anecdote of the time was how we won the Blockbuster account.

We had been working a number of years for Digital Equipment Company, also known as DEC. This was a large American company with offices around the world.

DEC had won the contract to supply Blockbuster Video stores throughout the UK with their point of sale hardware. In addition to winning the contract to provide the hardware, they also had the contract to maintain this equipment. Our role was to collect the new hardware from their various DEC stores and deliver the parts to their engineers working at Blockbuster outlets.

We had also been working for the last few years for ICL, another large plc supplying point of sale hardware, but in this instance, we were tasked with installing the hardware when we arrived on-site. Our drivers had been trained to enable them to do this work quickly, efficiently, and safely.

Drivers that had been trained were given the status of PT drivers, the PT standing for peripheral technicians. Not a name I ever liked, but one that ICL used, and they asked that we adopt the same terminology.

One day we were carrying out a straightforward delivery drop to a DEC engineer who was at the new Blockbuster store in Coventry. The store was so new it hadn't even opened to the public. The shop was being prepared for its big open day and my driver had arrived with a full vanload of boxes containing all the computer hardware needed. He was simply asked to place all the boxes in the corner of the shop.

The shop was a hive of activity with numerous members of staff filling shelves with films ready to be rented out, painters carrying out a final touch-up, carpenters finishing off the shop counters, cleaners trying their best to keep the mess to a minimum, and of course the DEC engineer trying to set up the tills. It was while my driver, who happened to be one of our PTs, was stacking the boxes in the corner of the room that he overheard the DEC engineer saying he couldn't get the scanner gun talking to the till.

On hearing this, my PT driver, who thought he knew what the problem might be, offered a suggestion to the man from DEC. Clearly rather put out by this remark, he was told, 'Well if you know so much about it, you fix it then!' So he did.

The branch manager, whose name was Jason, was extremely grateful and asked my driver for his name and which company he worked for, as he would like to ensure his services got recognition.

The driver was keen to relay the story when he got back to base, and I assured him I would let him know if I heard anything. I thanked him for a job well done.

Two days later I did receive a call from Jason thanking my company for the services provided, and in particular the help of one of my drivers. We got chatting and one thing led to another, the other being that Jason was not in fact the branch manager but one of the company's directors at Blockbuster. He had been at the branch to see how well it was preparing for its big open day.

We arranged to meet, and within six months the contract to maintain all the Blockbuster stores in the UK had been awarded to us. This was a huge coup and was one of the largest contracts we ever had.

Thankfully I had the foresight to advise DEC that one of their clients wanted to talk to me directly about maintaining the equipment. My contact at DEC was very relaxed about the whole situation and gave me his permission to meet with Blockbuster. Not that I needed his permission legally, but morally I thought it was the right thing to do. I also had the foresight to write to him thanking him for giving me that permission.

Once Blockbuster announced to DEC that they had lost the contract and it had been awarded to BXT, they went ballistic. I had the managing director from DEC on the phone, a man I had never spoken to before, wanting to know how I had the audacity to go behind their back. Thankfully, once I produced a copy of my letter showing I had done no such thing, the steam was taken out of the situation.

Okay, so my dinner party anecdotes may not trouble Billy Connolly, but I do bring good wine.

Yada, yada.

The trouble was, in addition to strengthening my management team to handle more responsibility and relieve some of the pressure I was under, I had the practical problem of finding more space to handle the additional Blockbuster work.

The solution was to expand our head office and depot at Aston with a nice new mezzanine floor, which is where I met Mark Holmes, the salesman from the company we chose to carry out the work. I liked him immediately.

After it had been completed and Mark came back to sign off on the job, I asked him if he would be interested in coming to work for me. I put together what I thought was an attractive salary package together with some generous additional benefits, like a top-of-the-range company car, a BMW 5 Series, extra holidays, and the big one, a share option in the company if he was still with me after three years. He jumped instantly.

I guess I saw something in him, something about trust and reliability that made him stand out, and I just felt instinctively he could be the answer to switching the company to a more management-run structure.

Just before Mark was due to start, I went out with friends for a meal at a Chinese restaurant in Lichfield. I had never been there before; it was well tucked away and far from where I usually went.

Sitting two tables away was Mark. I hadn't spoken to him since he had accepted the job, so I went over to him and introduced myself to the group. Funnily enough, he had never been to the restaurant before either.

Five years passed before I found myself back in the restaurant again, this time with a different group of friends. I was telling them the story of what happened the last time I was there, when one of them said, 'Wouldn't it be funny if he walked in tonight?'

As if on cue the door opened and Mark walked in with his new girlfriend. Their relationship was in its infancy and exciting, and he wanted to take her to somewhere nice and out of the way where they wouldn't know anyone.

Wrong!

Turned out he hadn't been back there for five years either.

A couple of weeks later I was out with my neighbours Peter and Jackie. Peter and I were having our usual catch-up on a Friday night discussing work. I sensed he was a little down and I asked him what was up. He told me he'd had an awful week at work. One of his long-time salesmen had just walked out on him without even giving notice. I know only too well what it's like to lose good people. It can unbalance the company for a while and take time for a new salesman to be accepted.

'Why did he leave?'

'Split up with his girlfriend.'

'Oh.'

'Yeah. Really hit him hard. She was lovely, but she fell for someone else. Evidently her new chap has more money, an amazing new job; he had shares in the company too, so it was more than just a hustle. He's also got a fab new company car, a BMW 5 Series. I think she said his name was Mark.'

'Oh!'

One more for the book, Dad.

# Chapter Twenty-three

They say you should never get on the wrong side of the taxman because they might carry out a formal tax inspection on you. If this happens, you're stuffed.

Tax inspectors are the SAS of the civil service. Ruthless, clever and take no prisoners.

Unless you're squeaky clean, and I mean squeaky clean, tax inspections are an expensive experience.

Luckily, I was squeaky clean. Not because I was an angel, simply that all work we undertook was for companies, and they wanted an invoice. We did no cash jobs so there was never the opportunity to have a little perk in the back pocket. Everything was correctly accounted for. Every job we carried out was invoiced, charged VAT, and went through the books. All payments went through the company's bank account, otherwise we wouldn't balance the ledgers at the end of each month.

Cool. No stress there then.

My personal tax situation was another story.

Maybe not so cool.

So is your mental image of a tax inspector the same as mine? Brown corduroy trousers, jacket with those 'maths teacher' patches over the elbows, woollen tie, braces, glasses, clumpy scuffed brown shoes?

No, no, no, no, no.

The guy who turned up on my door wore a sharp suit to match his sharp eyes.

Tax inspections are renowned for being wholly stressful, with the Inland Revenue working on the basis that they have right on their side. All the usual niceties of innocent until proven guilty get flung out the window, and they begin with the benchmark of, 'Mr Terry, in our eyes you are guilty until you can prove otherwise.'

Oh.

Let's explode some other tax inspection myths while we're here. You know the one about how they stick a pin in a telephone directory as a way of randomly selecting their next target? Doesn't happen. The Inland Revenue have to have a legitimate reason to suspect wrongdoing before they can carry out an inspection.

Once that inspection starts, watch out.

My company was used to having VAT inspections. These are carried out every two or three years, and to be honest were never an issue for me or my company. The accounts department was run extremely tightly and we did everything by the book.

Then we hit a depression – not mine, the company's. Well, the country's.

In 1989/1990 BXT was in financial trouble. The UK economy was in the deepest recession ever seen and I was finding it very hard to make a profit. I was fighting to keep my company afloat. Over those two years we lost £120,000, and it was the most stressful time of my life.

By the start of 1991, I had turned the company around and we were now back in the black. Yes of course cash flow was tight, as money was needed to re-invest in people and vehicles, but thankfully my new bank, Lloyds, had given me a lot of support. Still, it was hard times and I had to keep a very close eye on how much money was coming in and more importantly going out.

My accountants were a small family run firm based in Halesowen, on the outskirts of Birmingham. I had used them from the beginning and they produced my first full set of accounts for the year ending July 1978. The firm had been my dad's accountants and he had recommended them to me. I had always received a good, personal service from the senior partner, Andrew.

I think he liked the way BXT had grown over the years, and I was becoming one of his biggest clients.

Andrew's company specialised in helping self-employed people, like my dad, or small to medium-size businesses.

Maybe I had outgrown them.

After the 89/90 losses, my accountants could see that for the following year, ending 1991, it had been a good year and there was a significant turnaround in my fortunes. The company went from loss back into profit, but this meant a tax bill would soon follow.

Given the fact money was tight, Andrew advised me not to file 1991 year-end accounts on time. I had always filed within the time limits, but he advised I should delay. This would in theory cause the taxman to assess my anticipated profit and the Revenue would submit a tax demand based on that assessment. As the last two years had recorded a loss and the taxman had nothing else to go on other than those two previous years, they assumed I would have again made a loss.

There was no tax demanded.

My accountant did explain that when I eventually filed, albeit late, I would have to pay not only the corporation tax due but also that the Revenue would probably impose a small fine, plus added interest for late payment of tax. The tax due for that year was going to be around £20,000, so not paying it now was an attractive proposition.

My overdraft at the bank was already high and close to the limit. I thought it best to delay filing, pay no tax at the moment and keep what money I did have in the bank. Or, to be more truthful, keep what money I owed the bank on my overdraft as low as possible. Only when cash flow allowed would I submit my year-end accounts.

I knew the tax demand would then arrive pretty quickly after filing my accounts, but I would be in a much stronger position to pay it, plus any small fine and interest. All I had to do was keep BXT profitable and build up the reserves in my bank account. As my accountant put it, 'Better to borrow from the taxman than stretch the overdraft with the bank.'

It made sense, right up until I received a letter from the taxman saying they wished to have a meeting with me as a matter of urgency. I had by now paid the tax that was due, plus the interest, so I assumed it was for a telling-off.

He arrived, tall, middle-aged, dressed immaculately in a blue pinstriped suit.

Polite and methodical, he set about forensically investigating my affairs with all the studiousness of a pathologist on a murder case. Just for starters, he wanted to see copies of every personal bank and credit card statement I had going back over the past three years.

Also, the Revenue wanted to see invoices and receipts from all utility companies, but especially my home phone bill. I realise now they assumed my company had been paying it.

I was also asked to complete numerous forms saying how much I spent per month on things like food, clothes, holidays, gifts, charity donations, and more. I heard rumours that the taxman would ask you what you had for breakfast. It wasn't quite that detailed but not far off.

Finally, they made it clear that they reserved the right to go back further if necessary. Legally, they told me, they could go back up to six years.

Time to match their big guns with some of my own.

# Chapter Twenty-four

I didn't want to go back to my accountants as it was their advice that got me into this mess. I spoke to someone I knew at Deloitte & Touche. Deloitte were at the time one of the big five firms of accountants in the UK.

They'd been a client for some time, and we'd been running various documents and parcels around the UK for them. They dealt with large companies and corporations, but my contact was very helpful and recommended a chap called Tony. He had an excellent reputation. My contact at Deloitte thought I would get on well with Tony and he wasn't wrong on that score. Evidently, Tony had only recently set up his own practice in the last two years, so he was also hungry for new business. Deloitte told me he specialised in helping individuals like myself who were having to deal with Inland Revenue inspections.

He sounded perfect, and I knew I would like Tony immensely.

I called his number and after a very quick introduction explained my embarrassing predicament and we arranged to meet the next day. Tony explained he was indeed well placed to advise people in my position because, he had, up until two years ago, been a senior tax inspector himself. So gamekeeper becomes poacher, or should that be poacher becomes gamekeeper?

Mr Tax Inspector, I match your AK47 with one of my own. His name's Tony.

Our first meeting was at Tony's house over in Tamworth, which is a quaint small town about twenty miles north of Birmingham. Tony didn't have an office; he said he didn't need one as most of his meetings were at his clients' homes or places of work. Clearly, I had special privileges, and we sat around his large pine kitchen table. After some coffee and toast, we got down to talking tactics and how he felt the case would go.

Tony said he would write to the tax inspector who was overseeing the investigation to inform him that he was now acting for me and he would request copies of all future correspondence. He told me, with the certainty of inside knowledge, that they would not like this, but as I had given my authority they had no choice. Tony even knew who the senior inspector was, having worked with him on numerous occasions in the past. He told me he was one of the more senior inspectors based out of the Birmingham office and he did wonder why someone that high up would be put on my case. After all, I was hardly an Al Capone.

It was during the first meeting that Tony gave me some advice that I was not anticipating. For a second or two it floored me. He said, 'You need to come clean and confess anything and everything you have taken or enjoyed that the taxman could, and would, consider as being either income or a benefit in kind.'

I raised my eyebrows.

'I can only represent you if you are willing to do this.'

Naïvely I had anticipated Tony would say something like: think about what you have taken that you should have paid tax on, let me know, and I can tell you how we can get around it. Evidently it doesn't work like that.

Tony explained that I should not be in any doubt, the taxman would find any monies I had received or any benefits in kind I had enjoyed. If I confessed all my sins now, I would get up to eighty per cent discount on any fine, and a discount on the interest rate charged. If I didn't do this and they found something I hadn't admitted to, I would be fined and taxed on the amount at the going rate. There would also be a further tax equal to a penalty of one hundred per cent. So a tax of £1,000 becomes £2,000 plus a large fine. I was learning quickly. You don't want to mess with the taxman.

It was explained that I needed to forget about any guilt or embarrassment I felt. He said the inspectors do this work day in and day out and they are just not interested in judging people. He assured me that morals don't play a part in the taxman's psyche; all they are focused on is finding money that should have been taxed.

If I cooperated totally with the inquiry it would be completed much more quickly, and with a lot less stress. The sooner the investigation was over the quicker I could get back to concentrating on running my business.

It was good advice, and once I understood I would not be judged it became a lot easier. I agreed I would cooperate fully with the investigation.

I started to get all the documents together that the Revenue had asked for: receipts, credit card statements, and in particular my personal bank statements, all going back the last three years.

I had been asked to account for every single payment I had made into my personal bank account for the last three years. Thankfully, my own personal and company records were well kept.

I only had one personal current account with HSBC. I went through it meticulously. Every credit was shown in my statements.

The vast majority were easy to identify. Firstly, there was my salary, so that took care of thirty-six items (one payment per month for the last three years). Then there were any dividend payments I had received, again easy to find and explain. All these payments had the tax deducted at source.

Then I looked at any cheques I had banked. Once again, all of these could be accounted for. For example, a cheque from my insurance company for a small claim I had made. I was also able to provide supporting information, such as the letter from the insurance company.

Other small cheques paid in just after 24th March each year could be explained as they were birthday presents from members of my family and a few friends. They never knew what to get me so always gave me money, which was always great to receive.

Some items did take a little longer to work on. I didn't have paperwork to support them. For example, one time I paid for a holiday in full for me and my friends, who paid me back at a later stage. Luckily I had written on the paying-in stub and recorded what each payment was for. Tony assured me that as long as I submitted my stubs along with the statements they would accept what I was telling them. They are tough but not unreasonable, he said. ·

Some cash payments were a little harder to explain. I had the habit of throwing any loose change in my trousers when I got home into a jar, and about twice a year, I would bag this up and bank it. That was accepted by the Revenue.

Despite my best efforts, there were still some payments, amounting to approximately £1,000 over three years, that I just could not explain. These would only be small amounts, maybe £100 or £150 here and there. Try as I might, I had no recollection of where the cash had come from.

I had a further meeting with Tony and we went through everything I had collated. He was happy for me to send the bundle of information to the taxman.

I was fortunate that the majority of my spending was on a credit card. This gave me a detailed account of where I had spent my money and how much. So my food shopping bill, for example, was evident by my once a week visit to Sainsbury's. Also, any holidays, shopping for presents, shopping for clothes, dry cleaning bills, flights, etc. could all be shown. It was easy to see how much these items were and that I had paid off my credit bill each month, in full, from funds received from my salary.

I had to confess to Tony the things I had taken that I knew were wrong. He was surprised there were only two.

The first was easily resolved and we didn't have to confess to the taxman. I had bought a John Bampfield original painting a couple of years ago. He's an artist based down in Cornwall and I have always loved his work. In fact, I already had a couple of his paintings. This one, called Charge of the Light Brigade, had been hanging in my lounge at home. The problem was that I paid for it using a company cheque.

The following day, after I met with Tony, that picture was found hanging on my office wall at BXT. It remained there until I bought it back off the company, with the company even making a small profit, many years later.

The one thing I was not going to get away with was the fact my house was heated by domestic oil. I'd had oil delivered for the past two years by the same company who delivered the diesel to BXT. They would, at my request, send a separate invoice for the 'domestic oil' to my company and my company paid the invoice. The total amounted to just under £1,000, so certainly not a king's ransom. I did ask Tony if it was even worth confessing as it was unlikely they would come across these few invoices in my company's books.

This is where it helps to have a professional on your side.

'Where is your fuel tank at home?' he asked.

'At the side of my house.'

'Okay,' he said. 'Bet your life someone from the tax office will have already been down to your house to have a general look around. They will have noticed the fuel tank and at some point in the investigation they will ask you to provide not only the invoices for the domestic fuel you have used but also evidence of how you paid for it.'

I was beginning to see how the Revenue worked.

They had already asked me to confirm how much I spent on shopping each month, and of course, that was easy to prove because it was on my credit card statements. The fuel I had no answer for. Time to confess, Tony advised.

That's what I did. I admitted that I had rather foolishly paid for my domestic oil using a company cheque. This was a benefit in kind and I would now have to pay the tax on £1,000.

There were a few additional pieces of information the tax office asked me for. Normally, once a question had been asked, within twenty-four hours I had the answer and documentation to support my answer.

Tony assured me they would now be struggling to keep up because I was able to supply the information to them so quickly. This was, Tony said, very unusual.

I was also able to deliver any information they needed by courier, so there wasn't even a delay in the post. No sooner had they asked me for more information than it was on their desk the next day, sometimes the same day.

The investigation had been going on for around ten weeks. In that time the Revenue had visited my company twice, once at the beginning of their investigation, and then again a few weeks later when they set up camp for half a day compiling more information. Tony assured me this was standard practice but did add that the last inspection was only half a day and felt that was a good sign.

Following their last visit, I received a letter asking me to explain a flight paid for by the company. This flight, which was to Ireland, had been taken about two years previously. It was a flight from Birmingham Airport to Dublin.

I had absolutely no idea.

# Chapter Twenty-five

Not good,' Tony said.

He explained that the Revenue would now think they had found something. They could demonstrate a short flight had been paid for by BXT. They knew that we only did deliveries in mainland UK. Again I was getting to understand how the Revenue worked. I suspected they already had a copy of that flight information when they asked me the question. They were right, we did only make domestic deliveries, and they now thought that maybe I had taken a little jolly over to Ireland courtesy of BXT.

If I couldn't explain it, they would suspect there was more to be found.

'But I've never been to Dublin in my life,' I said.

Tony told me to mull it over and see if I could come up with anything. The Revenue had become used to me replying immediately to their queries, and I knew this delay in replying spoke volumes.

My memory was still blank, and I could find no explanation. As I say, I had up to now been answering queries within twenty-four hours, forty-eight at the most. A week had now gone by and I was still none the wiser.

It was annoying and I was stressed out.

Deciding to go to the office on Sunday morning when I knew everything would be quiet, I started to look at all the invoices we had raised around the same period as the flight to Dublin was taken. I knew the date of the flight and I knew it had been booked as a next-day return. I also knew it was midweek.

Suddenly I found what I had been looking for. Dad dance time... Woo-hoo!

How could I have forgotten? We had carried out a one-off special delivery for Digital Equipment Company, known as DEC. It was to deliver an urgent part to one of their engineers who was working in Ireland. I was not only able to produce a copy of our invoice to DEC for this one-off job, which clearly stated 'Delivery to Dublin', but I found a copy of the flight ticket in the name of one of my drivers. Best of all, I found in the DEC file a lovely letter from one of the directors thanking BXT for getting them out of a scrape.

I couldn't wait to tell Tony the news on Monday morning, and better still, I couldn't wait to send all the documentation, by courier, to the taxman.

Another couple of weeks went by. No more questions were forthcoming and Tony presumed the tax office themselves were stumped. They had found nothing, and Tony requested a meeting to discuss their findings and bring the investigation to a close.

Tony and I arrived at their offices, just off Colmore Row in Birmingham city centre. We waited in reception for a few minutes before being taken up some very wide stairs to the first floor and a meeting room, which Tony had been in many times. The man from the Revenue was waiting for us, and as we entered, Tony walked straight over and shook his hand. They looked like long-lost friends, and probably were. I shook the hand of the man who had been investigating me; the man who had been able to look so intensely and intimately into my private affairs. Our shake wasn't one of old friends.

After the usual pleasantries, we sat down at a huge dark wooden table, probably about twelve feet long by eight foot wide, with twelve leather chairs neatly and evenly spaced around it. The inspector sat on one side and Tony and I sat opposite. These were rather plush offices, I thought, looking around. Big solid doors, large sash windows, and what looked like oak panelling around the walls. The carpet was a rich deep red colour, and you could see it was expensive. The room was not particularly well lit, and the large brass lamps in two of the corners did not help throw up much extra light either. The whole room had a particular stuffiness about it, like being in an exclusive private member's club.

It was clear where some of my tax money had been spent.

Tony had pre-warned me that they use these offices to intimidate taxpayers. It was working.

The inspector, actually a nice man as it happened, thanked me for all the information I had provided and for my cooperation. He explained that following the investigation by his department, I was to be taxed on the £1,000 that I had estimated as the cost of the domestic oil paid for by my company.

By now I had actually found the invoices and added them up. I wasn't far out; it came to £930, but I wasn't about to argue over £70.

I was also to receive a small fine and a penalty for paying my tax late. The total proposed was £600.

He then went on to say that they had been pleased with the efficient way I had responded to their request for information and they saw I had cooperated fully. However, there was still the matter of approximately £1,000 in cash payments paid into my personal bank account over the last three years. As I could not account for these credits, he proposed charging me a further £400 in tax. This would bring my total tax and fine to a nice round figure of £1,000, and subject to payment being received by the Revenue, he was happy to close the case.

To me, it sounded like a deal, and I was ready to shake his hand there and then and get the hell out of this intimidating office. Tony asked for a few moments in private to discuss what had been proposed with his client, and we were shown into a small private room just off the main room.

'What do you think?' Tony asked.

'It's fine by me. Let's just pay it and get out of here.'

Tony agreed, and we re-entered the room where the inspector was still sitting on the other side of the big table.

We sat. Tony shuffled some papers, looked up and said, 'As you are fully aware, my client has cooperated fully with your investigation. Every request you have made for information or a verbal explanation has been provided in full and in a very timely manner. In all my years as an investigator, on both sides of this table, I have never witnessed any individual supply such detailed information with such clarity and speed. I am sure we can both agree this is very unusual and certainly makes a nice change. I have spoken to my client and we reject your proposal.'

What?!

'Although my client can't explain the cash of approximately one thousand pounds paid into his account, given this is over a three-year period, it only amounts to an average of £333 per year, a very small amount for my client given his earnings. He is adamant that it's not taxable. He is willing to pay the six hundred pounds mentioned, but not the additional four hundred, and if you object to this I can inform you now I will be escalating this to the area director as I believe it could be construed as harassment.'

Bloody hell, Tony.

The inspector looked taken aback.

I tried not to look the same.

We all stood up, shook hands, and Tony and I made our way out of the building.

Once we were outside on the pavement, I said, 'What just happened?'

'I was thinking you've done everything they asked for. There is no tax avoidance going on here so why should you pay an extra four hundred? My view is they will come back sometime early next week and settle for six hundred pounds. They certainly won't want me to escalate a complaint up the chain.'

A week later, as Tony predicted, I settled with a cheque payable to the Inland Revenue for £600 and the case was closed.

As a thank you, I took Tony out for a meal.

Holding up a glass of wine I said, 'Thanks, Uncle Tony.'

He grinned, chinked, and said, 'You're welcome.'

Actually, Tony was my girlfriend's uncle. Her dad's brother.

We all knew Uncle Tony was a tax inspector working for the ILR, but none of us knew that he had recently set up his own consulting business. It was only when Deloitte gave me his name that I knew it must be the same Tony, as the family has an uncommon surname.

One more for the book, Dad.

# Chapter Twenty-six

So here's the score: work was manic. I mean off-the-scale manic. Alongside that, profits were good. I was driving a good car: a Mercedes 320L. I had a lovely home, two gorgeous dogs, a pretty girlfriend, a fly-away place in Spain, and ate out whenever I wanted.

Sure I'd grafted for what I had, but I'm no fool, and I know I've had my fair share of luck along the way, mostly in the shape of coincidences that continued happening to me: 'Dad, it's happened again. Another one for the book!'

Coincidences had become part of my life, and I was beginning to see them as signposts either that I was on the correct path, or that I should switch to another.

Is that a form of luck, or something else? To be honest, I don't know any more.

All I do know is, they're there for me. So, with the company in profit and doing well, I felt that maybe it was time for me to be there for someone else. Give a little back. And, if there's a chance of a little publicity along the way, so much the better. You scratch my back and I'll pin a BXT logo on yours, so to speak.

Over the years BXT had sponsored many events, people and charities, including several parties, sponsored walks, a cycling team, a show jumper, a football team, and a ladies hockey team.

For the hockey team we paid for a new kit that proudly displayed the company logo on the back. My cousin Jane was a member, and one day she mentioned to me that their current sponsor had stopped supporting them and they needed a new kit. Not a very subtle hint, but I didn't mind and I was happy to help.

I was invited to the first match where they would be wearing it. I was a little surprised and disappointed when I first arrived to see that none of the girls were wearing the kit. They were all running around the playing field warming up in plain tracksuits. Ten minutes later, the referee blew her whistle and the teams were told to be ready to start in five minutes. They all dashed over to one corner of the field where their coach had been standing and I immediately recognised my logo on the back of the shirts now being taken out of a big cardboard box and distributed to the girls.

Off came the shirts they'd been wearing and on went the new, clean, crisp BXT logo'd shirts. I'd never seen so many bras on a Saturday morning.

There was no nice dressing room they could nip into to change, they just had to get on with it and strip off on the field. I could have understood if it was summer, but this was a cold, wet, miserable day. I was already freezing, even with my big woollen coat on. However, they won. I think. I wasn't sure. I'd never seen a hockey match before and wasn't sure how to score it, but they looked happy when they came off.

Another sponsorship close to my heart was for a young chap who was into his Formula Ford racing. His team manager, better known as his dad, had phoned me out of the blue asking if my company would be interested in helping and supporting his son, Mark Bryan. I would be given the opportunity to have our company logo plastered across the side of his Formula Ford single-seater racing car. This had several benefits from my point of view. First and foremost, we would be helping a young lad and his dreams. Secondly, the connection with the speed of his car in a race and what services my own company provided was not lost on me. Thirdly, I was promised a go in the car the next time they were doing a practice session at Donington Park race track in Leicestershire.

It was the final offer that helped clinch the deal, and for twelve months we helped towards the running costs.

After that year was up, they asked if I'd continue with the sponsorship. To be honest it was getting expensive, but what tipped the balance was something in the driver's eyes that I recognised from my own, that steely determination to succeed against the odds. I liked that, that sense that nothing was going to stop him. So I said yes.

Soft hearted, maybe. But businessman... always.

It had been announced that Formula Three racing, one down from Formula One, was coming to the streets of Birmingham, and the Formula Fords were to be on the bill as a support race. I figured it could do no harm at all to see my logo whizzing by.

This was the first time street racing was to be been seen in the UK. Birmingham was trying to become the next Monte Carlo, except without the harbour, luxury yachts, casinos, sun or money. All minor points.

It put an energy into the step of Birmingham, and most people were looking forward to it. The event was due to take place during the May bank holiday. It was to be known as the Birmingham Superprix, and included Formula Ford 1600 and Formula 3000 racing. Not as catchy as Monte Carlo or bust, but it had a ring to it none the less.

The very first race of the day would be the Formula Ford cars. Our man Mark had made it into the final, an amazing achievement considering many of the teams had big-name sponsors you'd recognise from Formula One plastered all over the car and shirts of the pit crews.

Formula Ford is a feeder series into the bigger formulas, and everyone was on the lookout for the next Senna, Prost or Mansell. The buzz was palpable.

Of course, I had grandstand tickets. I wasn't going to miss this for the world.

Yeah, but I kind of wish I had.

Britain decided it couldn't compete with the Monte Carlo weather, so decided to do its own thing and pissed down. Hurricane Charley they called it. Charley, Charley, Charley, of all the days!

It was a miracle there was any racing at all, but just before the start of the first race, the weather gods went, 'Okay, seeing as you put so much effort in, go on then,' and eased the rain, not all the way, but enough to get the green light.

It was cold and wet, and the track was super slippery, with everyday Birmingham oil, diesel and the odd doner kebab all ground into the tarmac.

We took our positions in the grandstand opposite the start/finish line. Craning my neck, I could see our boy towards the back of the grid. I wondered how he felt on his home grand prix, and sent him all the good vibes I could.

Ready, steady, GO!

The chequered flag went down.

The crowd erupted.

And they were off.

For Mark, quite literally.

First corner.

To be fair the spray from the cars was ridiculous, and as they whooshed by they even soaked the first three rows in the grandstand, so goodness knows what it must have been like for the drivers out there.

Go, Go, Go!

The cars roared off down to the first left-hand corner, the garbled commentary coming from the speakers and the cheers from the crowd adding to the thrill.

As they sped away, the noise from the cars quietened as they raced up Belgrave Middleway towards the first hairpin at Haden Circus, with the commentator announcing, 'Such a shame for Mark Bryan, who crashed on the first corner, but the good news is he is okay and the car looks to be all right.'

First race, first crash, first to be out. Not the first any of us was hoping for.

Within a few minutes the roar of the cars returned as they once again entered the top of Bristol Street and headed past the start and finish line in front of us. Lap one complete, only eleven more to go.

The following day, the front page of the Birmingham Post and Mail showed a picture of Mark's Formula Ford car being hoisted into the air by a big crane and plonked to the side of the circuit. It was a spectacular photo, and I smiled at the BXT logo on the side of the car.

We were not the only sponsor of Mark's car. The main sponsor had been Wimpey Homes. The area director of Wimpey had also been there, and I met him after the race. We chatted about how well Mark had done to even get into the competition, and how proud we were of him.

We exchanged business cards, and shortly after, Wimpey became clients, proving the age-old adage, All's Well That Ends Well, Even if You Do Bin It on the First Bend.

# Chapter Twenty-seven

Baggage is a word that has a bad rep. 'How's your new boyfriend?' 'Don't! He has baggage!'

But I like the word. It's accurate. It feels to me like you go through life with a suitcase that you fill with all your personal experiences and emotions, fears and elations, sadness and hilarity. Once it's in the suitcase, you can never get rid of it. It becomes part of you.

My baggage was crammed corner to corner with work. Sure there were some other bits and pieces in there, but if you'd opened it and snuck a look inside, you'd see BXT.

However, it felt like that was changing.

It felt like, I don't know... It felt like I was discovering life.

No, that's wrong. It felt like I was discovering fun.

Work was still the predominant factor in my world, and I knew at some point I had to delegate more, as scary as that felt, but it also felt like I was now adding other things to my baggage, related but also unrelated to work. And that felt good. Healthy, you know?

Cut to a summer ball at the prestigious Grosvenor House Hotel in London. This was in aid of a fantastic charity called Starlight Children's Foundation. They make wishes come true for children with limited life expectancy. Honestly, some of the stories would break your heart. The event was organised by Blockbuster Video, one of my clients.

'Nick, you will come, won't you?' Jason, my man at Blockbuster, said.

'Of course!' And I confirmed I'd take two tables of ten. All I had to do now was find nineteen people to join me.

In reality, this was easy. For the first table of ten I had invited some of my close friends, and for the second table I invited some of my clients. It was a nice mix of people, and for once I could relax and let my hair down.

After a splendid meal, and before the dancing started, there was to be an auction. This was a star-studded event with some big names dotted around some of the other tables. The auctioneer was Jeremy Beadle, and the prizes up for auction were all one-off-money-can't-buy items.

It was coming towards the end of the auction, and up to now I had managed to sit on my hands, because I'm in the habit of getting slightly carried away at these events.

Jeremy announced that the CEO of Blockbuster had flown over from the States to be at the event and had donated a boxing glove to the auction that he had owned for a few years. This was no ordinary boxing glove, it was a real one-off. The red boxing glove was displayed inside a large wooden case with a glass front and was brought on the stage for people to view. Jeremy read out the names of boxers, all of whom had signed the glove. George Foreman, Ken Norton, Joe Frazier, Larry Holmes, Mike Tyson, Lennox Lewis, Evander Holyfield, Riddick Bowe, and the greatest of them all, Muhammad Ali. Signatures of nine of the most famous heavyweight boxers of the world. Wow, what a prize! Time to release my hands I thought.

The bidding went up, and up, and up, and up, until there were only two people in the room left bidding, me and Hugh Grant.

I didn't think I stood a chance. I had in my mind the maximum I would pay and kept telling myself two things: it's a great cause, and oh boy wouldn't this look good on my office wall at home.

Jeremy was on good form and had already persuaded me to go higher than I wanted. As usual I was getting carried away.

I had reached my limit a few bids previously and knew for definite I had to stop. Hugh Grant had again bid a further £1,000 over and above my last bid, and sadly I had to shake my head. I knew when I was beat. The hammer crashed down with a great thud and there was a warm round of applause for the victor.

I was disappointed but pleased to have played my part in helping raise some extra money for such a great charity.

After the auction was over I made my way over to Hugh's table. He was sitting next to Stephen Fry. Intimidated? Me? God, yes!

I could see the wooden case containing the boxing glove by his feet, and gingerly approached him to congratulate him on his winning bid.

'Oh, was it you I was bidding against?' he said.

'Yes,' I admitted. 'I'm afraid I got a little carried away. I was wondering if you would mind if I could have a quick look at it?'

He couldn't have been more friendly and pleasant, and even Stephen Fry joined in our conversation. I really was mixing with the stars, well for a couple of minutes anyway.

'Are you into boxing then?'

'Not particularly, but the thought of owning a one-off glove like this certainly appealed to me.' Appealed to me? What sort of language was I speaking? Just relax. And breathe. That last one's quite important: the breathing thing.

Hugh then made me an offer that rather stunned me for a second. 'How much did you bid up to?'

I told him.

'Okay. If you're still prepared to pay that to the charity, then I am more than happy to let you have it.'

Wow!

Hang on a minute. Here he was getting the round of applause and the accolade for being the highest bidder, was he now welching on the deal?

Much as I wanted the glove, it felt all wrong.

'That's very kind of you, Mr Grant—'

'Call me Hugh.'

'—but if we do that, the charity would be down by a thousand pounds.' Which was the difference between our final bids.

'No, you misunderstand, I have already given them my money. I don't want it back. But if you now pay what you had bid, they double their money, don't they?'

They do. They do indeed. What a true gentleman and kind guy.

So that's what we did. Hugh said he knew someone who worked for Blockbuster, and after a quick look around the room he saw him, caught his eye, and beckoned him over to the table. That someone just happened to be my old friend Jason, who had just renewed the Blockbuster contract with me.

The deal was done and the following week I sent my cheque. Jason then called me a few days later to say the glove was ready for collection, adding, 'Do you know a reliable courier that could come and collect it?'

Funny man!

The boxing glove still hangs on my office wall at home, and every time I look at it I smile.

But if we're rummaging through the baggage of my life, the proudest moment is undoubtedly when the Bishop of Birmingham asked if we'd deliver the books of condolence to London that had been signed by the people of Birmingham in memory of Princess Diana.

In total there were five very large leather-bound books, and we had been asked to deliver them to Buckingham Palace. It was a great honour but also a great responsibility.

I arranged for two vans to take the books, one to carry them and the other to shadow the first driver in case of any problems. I had nightmares of the first van breaking down, or, worse, having an accident resulting in us failing to deliver. The headline 'BXT does not deliver' splashed across the newspapers would be more than I could handle.

However, it went without a hitch.

Phew.

Then there's the other baggage. The not so nice stuff that leaves a bad taste in your mouth.

On the whole the people who worked for me were diligent and loyal. But we did have a few bad apples.

When I began to employ van drivers, as opposed to the self-employed motorcycle couriers, I had to find a way for them to fill up with fuel when they were out on the road. In those early days, we issued everyone with company Access cards. The forerunner of MasterCard. Access had a slogan, Access, Your Flexible Friend.

Well, one of my drivers took that to heart.

Back in the early 1980s, petrol stations latched on to the idea of selling more than engine-related products, realising that as a matter of convenience we'd happily buy a few home essentials along with a tank of fuel.

One of the forerunners in my neck of the woods was the BP garage on Harborne Lane, between Selly Oak and Harborne. One of my drivers thought he was onto a nice little scam by adding his own weekly shop for groceries to his half tank. The fool of a driver even boasted to the cashier that his company was paying for all his shopping and they didn't even know about it.

You needed a bit of luck in business. Fortunately for me, the manager of the petrol station who happened to be serving on the till that day had noticed, and he remembered the name of the company on the side of the van. The following week, when my dad called at his house to collect the monthly rent for the TV he was renting to him, he asked my dad, 'Doesn't your son run a courier company called BXT?'

'He does. What made you say that?'

He told him.

Dad immediately phoned me. It only took a couple of minutes to go through the receipts and work out which driver it was.

The following morning I sacked him.

'You can't do that!'

I also told him I was keeping back his last two week's wages.

'You can't do that either!'

It was good fortune for me that of all the petrol garages he chose to rip me off in, it was one where the manager knew my dad.

If I'd had the boxing glove back then I might even have boxed his ears.

# Chapter Twenty-eight

Life's all about learning lessons. Lessons ensure you're growing, and to be successful in business, you must grow.

Every day's a school day.

After the driver used the company credit card to stock up his fridge, I became a bit more wary. I thought about recalling all the credit cards, but then how would drivers get fuel?

If that wasn't an option, maybe there was a middle ground.

That solution involved installing a diesel tank in the yard. At least then they could fill up on-site before heading out. They'd still have to have a card for emergencies when they were too far from base and running low, but it mitigated the risk.

We also swapped over to Allstar Fleet Fuel Cards, which had a restriction that only fuel could be bought. You couldn't even get a sneaky newspaper added to your purchase. It even recorded the registration number of the vehicle.

It would be naïve for me to think it would never happen again, but we had enough safeguard systems in place now to ensure any little fiddle was very minimal.

We even restricted how much fuel could be purchased at any one time using the Allstar cards to ensure vans got refilled at the base as much as possible. It was also a heck of a lot cheaper.

However, some people will always try and do a fiddle for a few extra quid.

All that was backed up by our brilliant accounting system under the watchful eyes of Amanda, who worked for me for eight years, and then Veronica, who worked for me from 1990 to the sale of the company.

Every week Veronica would present me with a summary draft report on how each branch was running, and then at the end of every month a much more detailed report showing how the company was doing overall.

One of the things my weekly reports showed me was the cost of fuel per week per branch. I would also get a note showing how much the fuel had cost as a percentage of the turnover.

I had begun to notice that the fuel cost, as a percentage of Birmingham's turnover, was steadily creeping up. I couldn't just take one week's reading on its own because there would always be some fluctuation, but over a few weeks I could see things didn't look right. Given the fact that the cost of fuel had remained steady, the percentage measured against turnover should have remained fairly constant. I was beginning to think something was amiss. If my figures told me something wasn't right, my gut screamed something was decidedly iffy.

I continued to monitor the use of fuel out of the Birmingham depot and watched it rise way above expected usage, and concluded either every driver had invested in heavy hobnail boots to drive in, or someone was on the rob.

Clearly, I needed to do something.

Without telling a soul, I arranged to have a concealed camera installed in the yard so I could see what was going on.

The yard was on the side of our building next to double shutters that led into the warehouse. The warehouse was made up of various storage bays, some for general clients, some for individual clients. Those clients with high-value items had their own locked storage rooms. We had a large meeting room and a workshop used to repair point of sale equipment for my largest client, Blockbuster Video. Above those rooms was a mezzanine floor for additional storage.

The company had grown so much over the past few years that the management team had also been expanded to help with the efficient running of the business, and of course with extended management you need offices for them all to work in.

The structure was set up as such: on the ground floor there was a drivers' waiting room which, like the good old days from Thorp Street, had a hatch into the main operations room. Some things never change. The central operations room remained the heart of the business and was always bustling with excitement and noise, with calls coming in, drivers going out, and general organised mayhem.

A separate room housed another call centre for handling only Siemens Computers jobs, which by comparison was always a sea of calm.

There was a small kitchen used by all with the usual facilities you would find, including a fridge, toaster, a microwave, TV, hot and cold drinks machine, and a vending machine, which annoyingly for my diet dispensed small packs of chocolate Hobnob biscuits which I could never resist. I would often walk into this room and spend a few minutes with various members of staff to have a chat and get a feel for how things were. It was also the room with the comfiest chairs.

Now we even had three toilets: one for male drivers, one for female drivers, and one executive toilet for the sole use of senior staff – trust me, you would not want to use the loo after some of those drivers!

The branch manager Matt, who probably had one of the hardest jobs, had his own office, although most of his day was spent in the operations room. I certainly missed the buzz of running the ops room. It was always a very stressful job, but you got a huge sense of satisfaction when at the end of the day all the deliveries had been completed on time.

The company had grown so much by now we even employed a full-time human resources officer. Jenny had her own ground-floor office opposite the drivers' room. Any staff member could nip in and address any issue they might have, which must have made her life hell but she was so efficient you'd never know it.

Upstairs on the first floor were the senior staff, plus the accounts department run by Veronica and assisted by Alison and Becky.

Jim and Carol looked after key accounts, and along the corridor was Terry, my general manager. Next to Terry's office was Mark the sales director.

I had my own office, which due to its size could double up as a meeting room, and I was supported by my PA, Eileen, in her adjoining office.

It gives me goosebumps to think how far the company had come from the days of running it out of my bedroom with a map pinned to the wall and a telephone I'd have to leave off the hook when I went out on delivery.

The new surveillance camera was installed along with a monitor hidden under my desk. Now I'd be able to see why the fuel costs were spiralling.

As soon as it was in, I came clean to my PA and the other directors, Mark and Veronica. Other than that, it was secret squirrel.

I'd be a liar to say it wasn't quite exciting.

On the Monday night after the installation, I was chilling with Champ and Rebel at home wondering what I'd find recorded in the morning, when the phone rang.

I looked at the time. It was ten o'clock.

Unless you're newly in love or have a best friend in Australia, late-night phone calls are never good.

'Hello?'

'Nick? It's Keith.'

'Blimey, Uncle Keith. How are yo— Oh God, Dad. Is something wrong with Dad?'

'No, no, no. He's fine. At least I think he's fine. Was last time I spoke to him anyway. No, this is about your work.'

'My work?'

'Yes. You see…'

For the last three months or so Keith had been doing a bit of casual work as a black cab driver in Birmingham. He had taken a course, passed his exam, and was earning good money working a night shift. An old school friend of his owned a cab but only liked to work a daytime shift, so rather than have his expensive machine sitting on his drive at night, he rented it to my Uncle Keith.

He went on to say that while he was taking a break at a night café frequented by black cab drivers, he overheard one of the drivers boasting that he knew where cabs could fill up with cheap diesel. He heard them say that the going rate was twenty-five per cent discount off the best pump price, for cash.

Uncle Keith asked about this little scam but he was told it was restricted to just a few drivers as they didn't want to overcook the goose. However, we all know how black cab drivers like to gossip, and within thirty minutes Keith had established that the place to get cheap fuel was a courier company called BXT.

It all rang horribly true.

I thanked him and promised to catch up soon – I hadn't seen him in forever.

I didn't sleep much and was at the office before the birds had even started singing. The night manager had yet to clock off from his shift.

There was nothing unusual about my early start. Except... today there was.

In my office I got the monitor out from under my desk and viewed the night's recording. Of course, I knew what I was going to see, but it was still unpleasant viewing and gave me a real knot in my stomach. The previous night at ten thirty, and again at just after three, a black cab pulled into the yard. Both times, my night manager – a big chap, we'll call him John – could be seen coming out of the side door and filling the cabs with my fuel. The camera even captured the moment he was handed cash from the taxi drivers. Priceless footage.

I had already asked my night manager not to leave that morning as I wanted to speak to him, but first I needed to wait until Terry Chapman, my general manager, had arrived at work, as I felt he should sit in on the meeting.

It's always best to have a witness.

Terry, who was never late for work, arrived just before eight and waved at me through the small glass window of my office door as he walked past. I buzzed him on our internal phone system and asked him to join me in my office. I explained what was going on and we watched the video footage together, I still had knots in my stomach.

The morning operation staff had arrived so I buzzed down to Matt, my branch manager, and asked him if he could find we'll-call-him-John and send him up.

We'll-call-him-John knocked and walked in.

Is it my imagination or did he look sheepish?

I asked him if he knew anything about taxis, particularly black cabs, coming into the yard and filling up with diesel from our fuel tank?

He had a blank expression, followed by a look of surprise, and then he settled on a look of cherub-like innocence. 'Er no. I don't know anything about that. Why, what's going on, boss?'

The boy should have been an actor.

I produced the monitor from under my desk and the three of us watched the video in silence.

When it finished he said, 'Okay, fair cop. But it was only just the once and I'm happy to pay you back.'

I knew it wasn't and told him so.

Then I sacked him.

'You can't do that!'

Now where had I heard that line before?

He was owed a month's wages and ten days' holiday.

But he wasn't getting it.

'You can't do that either!'

I'm sorry but is there a parrot in here, or does everyone who's been sacked say the same thing?

'Yeah, well sue me.' Oh I do like that line.

I suspect from the information on my internal accounts that the scam had been going on for a little while, so I don't think he was too much out of pocket.

I never heard from him again.

# Chapter Twenty-nine

How far away from the BBC are you?'

Now that's not a sentence you hear very often. The BBC studios are at Pebble Mill, in Edgbaston, not a handful of miles away, I told the caller.

'Excellent! Can you handle an urgent collection and delivery today?'

It was Saturday morning, and while I could palm the weekend jobs off, I tended to do them myself because I liked driving and it was cheaper. Plus they tended to be a bit quirkier than your weekday work.

'Oh yes!'

Sigh. 'Thank goodness. Please collect from Pebble Mill and deliver to Noel Edmonds' house.'

'I think I can handle that.'

She gave me the addresses to both and hung up.

Noel Edmonds. Part of me was surprised he had a home so far away from a television studio, he was on the screen that often. His current show was Telly Addicts. I suspected it was a script or something to do with that.

I wondered what his house was like. Grabbing my jacket and keys, I headed off to find out.

The collection was simple, the package waiting for me in reception. Outside, I looked at the delivery address, a place not far from Farnham.

In those days there were no satnavs, so you had to rely on a map book, a sense of direction and the confidence to ask for directions.

Thankfully his place was easy to find, and I arrived at a set of rather imposing black wrought-iron gates, both flung open to reveal an enormous, beautiful house beyond.

There was a buzzer to the side. I wandered over and pressed it, turning to take in the wall and trees that flanked his pad. It was all super impressive.

I expected to hear a voice instructing me to leave the parcel, with an added, 'Thank you my man, your work here is done.' Which would have been a shame as I really wanted to see more.

So I gave it a very long two seconds, turned and legged it back to the van.

The drive was sweeping. You've got to have proper money to have a drive that sweeps.

Around the first bend I could see his house in front of me. It looked like it would have been a large manor house in its day. The hard-core drive changed to gravel as I got nearer to the house. Out front was parked a brand-new Range Rover.

Slipping in behind it, I left the vehicle and made my way to the front door, set in a lovely old porchway. There was a bell to the side. Reaching up, I pressed it.

I heard it ring inside the house.

I waited… and waited. Then I pressed it again. Still nothing.

I looked for a letterbox but couldn't see one. Besides, I needed a signature.

I pressed it again.

Still nothing.

Deciding I needed to be more proactive, I began walking down by the side of the house and the fence that ran beyond it, looking for a way around the back. I could hear sounds of life, if the noise of a tractor counts as life.

Soon I found a gate. It wasn't locked. Turning the handle, I pushed it open to reveal a small courtyard along with one Noel Edmonds on a bright red Massey Ferguson 125, loading and shifting some wooden pallets that were stacked on the front forks of the tractor.

He saw me straight away, and to be honest he looked a little fraught, as he must have been thinking, 'Who the bloody hell is this walking through my gate?'

He turned the engine off and jumped down from the cab. It's true what they say you know. He really isn't very tall.

Keen to disarm the situation and assure him my intentions were honourable, I gave him my best, 'Good afternoon,' and explained I had an urgent document from the BBC in Birmingham for his attention, and I needed a signature.

A little more relaxed now, he signed my paperwork. I thanked him and left. Nice man, nice car, and a nicer house.

Known for his love of cars, I wondered what treasures he might have squirrelled away.

I loved my cars too, and as the company was buying around a hundred new vans a year, I had pretty good buying power, and as such I found it was easy for me to get a good deal with the motor manufacturers or their dealerships. They would be keen to secure the business for the commercial vehicles, and in return, I was able to take advantage of securing a great deal on my personal company car. When things were hot, I was changing my car every year. It was great fun. Because of this, I was known to all the dealers.

One day I got a call from the head of sales at Citroen asking if I would like to attend the launch of their new flagship saloon car, the Citroen C5. My initial thought was that it wasn't for me, but he went on to say the launch was to take place in Monte Carlo and it would be a two-night stay at the prestigious Loews Hotel, all expenses paid. Well you know what, I think I might be interested after all.

So I flew off to Monte Carlo for what turned out to be a fantastic trip. Everything had been laid on and clearly no expense was spared. The most amazing thing was when our plane, which had been chartered by Citroen, landed at Nice airport we were shown to a fleet of coaches awaiting us at the bottom of the plane's steps. We had a police escort to our first destination which turned out to be a wonderful coastal restaurant somewhere between Nice and Monte Carlo with a splendid lunch laid on.

It was only afterwards that I realised that at no time did customs ask to see any of our passports. We were just whisked straight out of the airport and onto the highway. I guess Citroen, being a very large French company, has a lot of influence with the authorities.

After a lovely lunch we were driven to our hotel and we all checked in. We had been told that dinner would be served in one of the main dining halls within the hotel at eight, but to make our way there a little earlier in our best black-tie get-up.

There must have been twenty tables of ten, all laid out with the finest white linen, silver cutlery and crystal wine glasses. The food was fabulous, accompanied by the best French wine the country could produce.

After a brief speech by the chairman of Citroen, who confirmed that tomorrow we would get the chance to test drive their latest new car, we were encouraged to relax and enjoy the evening. The entertainment was provided by the group The Three Degrees, and our host for the evening was none other than Noel Edmonds, whose house I'd been to the week before.

As the evening moved on I watched Noel work the room, stopping at each table for a chat. Of course, when he arrived at our table he asked us if we were all having a good time. I managed to catch his eye and with a wide grin said, 'Were you on a little red Massey Ferguson 125 last weekend moving some wooden pallets around?'

He really was flummoxed.

In hindsight it would have been much funnier if I'd left it at that, but I didn't and I explained it was me who'd delivered the envelope from the BBC to him last weekend.

The look on his face was priceless.

Sunday night it was time to pack up, and I had to rush. I had tickets to Gloria Estefan that night. What a weekend it was turning out to be.

# Chapter Thirty

Sometimes I wonder how much I missed out on. Hey, this is just cards on the table time, and don't get me wrong, I'm happy with the decisions I made, but in the same breath I wouldn't be human if I didn't have the odd passing thought that mumbled, 'What would your life have been like if you hadn't been so driven to succeed?'

It's the business equivalent of a couple's pillow talk: 'So what would your life have looked like if we hadn't met?'

If I'd never met BXT, what would my life have looked like?

Hand on heart answer, the same.

If it hadn't been BXT, it would have been something else with the same result. I feel like I'm the product of me. Does that make sense? I've achieved the life I set out to get, and the one I was meant to have. Ever since I sat in that church aged eleven thinking about Dick Whittington, and then the school careers officer asked what I wanted to do when I grew up and I answered honestly that I wanted to be a millionaire, I've been on this path. Yet it wasn't the easy one. Far from it. And yeah, I missed out on a lot along the way.

Which is why, as I was approaching forty and beginning to feel the heavy weight of work fatigue, fun was factored much more in my decisions.

Can we make it from Birmingham Airport to the NEC to watch Gloria Estefan? Maybe, if everything went to schedule.

So let's see, the plane from our fab Citroen weekend in Monte Carlo would touch down at Birmingham Airport at seven, and Gloria was due on stage at eight. With a two-minute shuttle ride and a five-minute walk in between, it would be a piece of cake.

Piece of cake, I tell you!

Unless, of course, the plane was delayed taking off, which it was. Of course it was.

Arrival was now due at eight fifteen, a whole quarter of an hour after Gloria had swooshed out in front of her thousands and thousands of fans looking and sounding amazing.

Resigned to the fact that I'd miss the beginning, I concentrated on rushing the bits I could influence.

I dashed into the arena showing my tickets and apologising for being late.

'Don't worry,' the lady said, smiling warmly. 'Follow me, I'll take you to your seats.'

I'd managed to secure third row centre seats with a fantastic view, so the walk was right the way down to the front. As we got close it became obvious that another couple had already taken our seats. To me, it was clear what had happened. This couple had noticed that these two seats, right near the front with great views, had not been taken and had pinched them.

Fair play, but they had to understand when we turned up that they'd have to vacate.

The security lady flashed her torchlight in their direction and eventually caught their attention. They were duly summoned to get up and come and talk to security, who at this stage was standing at the end of the row in the middle walkway. Everyone from the middle seat to the last seat on the side had to stand up so these wicked people could make their way out to the end of the row. I was extremely aware we were causing a right rumpus, but thankfully there was no stopping Gloria and she continued singing as though nothing was happening. I feel sure she must have been aware of the commotion.

Once the couple had managed to make their way to the end of the row, we were told by the security lady to take our seats. I gave her my best smile, thanked her, and we made our way to the seats which were rightly ours.

Again everyone in the row had to stand to allow us to pass, and I was saying sorry to everyone as we passed, repeating, just loud enough for them to hear, 'Sorry, but they were in our seats.'

We sat down, and at last, after all the rushing around, I could settle back and enjoy the concert I'd been so looking forward to.

I had only been in the seat for less than thirty seconds when I became aware of a flashlight in my eye. It was the security lady requesting we vacate our seats and head towards her. What on earth was going on now? Yet again everyone had to stand, and I would not have blamed Gloria one bit if she stopped the concert while these fools sorted themselves out.

When I got to the end of the row the security woman asked to see my tickets again. She shone her light down, paused for a second, and then said, 'These tickets are for tomorrow night.'

I could have died.

The couple whom I had glared at when we swapped places now quite rightly threw me daggers.

'I am so sorry,' I said to the security lady, who seemed to find it all highly amusing.

'Have you come far?' she asked.

I was so flustered I said, 'I've just flown in from Monte Carlo.'

Clearly mortified, she offered a spot in the disabled area to watch the concert from there.

'That's very kind,' I said, 'but I think we will come back tomorrow night.' And with my tail firmly between my legs, my head bowed low, I did the walk of shame out of the arena.

Okay, so of course I can laugh about it now. I was a bloody idiot for getting the dates wrong. It was a mistake, and we all make them. But hidden under that bravado was the sense that I was missing details.

Twenty years ago I would not have got the dates wrong.

So following my rather disastrous visit to the NEC Arena to see Gloria Estefan, I wanted to ensure my next visit, many years later, went without a hitch. I made sure I was going to turn up on the right day, always a good start. On this occasion, I had tickets to see Leona Lewis in concert. About eighteen months earlier, she had won season three of The X Factor. Not wishing to take away anything from the other winners who had gone before or after, but to me she was in a class of her own. I had managed to secure two tickets with good seats with a three-course meal included, which was at one of the many restaurants within the arena itself.

When Diane and I first arrived we went to check exactly where our seats were as I didn't want to be agitated looking for our seats after our meal. Having located our seats, we then went off to find the restaurant. Diane spotted a sign with our restaurant's name and an arrow pointing upward. So, following the sign, we took a flight of stairs to the first floor and entered through the double doors and stood, as instructed, next to a podium and another sign saying 'Please wait here to be seated'. They do like their signs at this arena! A few seconds later we were approached by a smartly dressed young man who asked us for our names and how many of us was in our party. I did feel tempted to do an over-the-top glance around looking for other people as it was clear for all to see there was just the two of us. I think Diane instinctively knew what I was thinking because she grabbed my hand and squeezed it really tightly, as if to say, don't you dare even think about it! I didn't dare, and instead I politely replied, 'Oh it's just the two of us tonight.' We were then informed that all the tables for 'two' had been taken and asked if we were happy to take a table set up for four, but we were advised that we might have two strangers join us. Well, I wasn't happy but what could I do? We were shown to our table and I ordered some drinks and our choice of starters.

Just as our starter course arrived I saw a waitress moving in our direction with two people. Complete strangers! They introduced themselves and apologised for having to join us, adding that they had actually booked a table for two. 'So had we,' I replied.

As it turned out they were a super couple, about our own age, and the conversation flowed easily. We decided not to watch the support act, staying instead to enjoy the company of our new friends. I called the waitress over to order another bottle of wine. I have a pet hate about sitting in my car in a long queue at the end of a concert waiting to get out of the carpark, so I had already booked a room at the Marriott Hotel, which was within walking distance. So another bottle of wine, or two, would be fine. No driving home for me tonight thank goodness.

The waitress took my order but said she would clear away the empty dishes on the table. While she was doing this we carried on chatting and, having been asked the question, I started to explain that I ran my own courier company called BXT.

The waitress nearly dropped the dirty plates in my lap. 'Excuse me,' she said, 'but I couldn't help overhearing. Are you Nick Terry, by any chance?'

'Yes I am,' I said.

'Oh, my brother works for you. His name's Dean, do you know him?' she asked.

Well what a small world. Of course I knew Dean, he had been working for me for around five years. She went off, and when she returned with my bottle of wine, she whispered to me, 'It's on the house.' I'm not sure she was meant to do that, but it was a kind gesture and I made sure she received a nice tip.

The support act finished and an announcement was made over the speakers to say Leona Lewis would be on stage in five minutes and we should take our seats. We all stood up, said our goodbyes, and that was that. I needed to pop to the loo so I was a little late getting to our seats, but well before Leona appeared on stage, not 'late' like the Gloria Estefan concert! It was only then as we made our way to our seats that we found our new friends from the restaurant sitting next to us. The arena has 15,685 seats according to Google. What were the chances? Well in this case 1 in 15,685, or 1 in 7,843 if you consider there were two seats, but who's counting!

Two weeks later I was relaying this story to some friends, David and Sue, and they started to laugh and told me that their friends had been to the exact same concert, and they also had to share a dining table with a couple they didn't know. The chap ran a courier company and when they went to watch the concert, the same couple from the restaurant had seats next to theirs. Honestly, you couldn't make it up.

Forty was always the age at which I wanted to retire, and as that birthday drew closer, the feeling that I was having to work harder and harder to keep up wasn't lost on me. I was exhausted, shattered and pooped.

Luckily, work was pretty streamlined, and with the management team taking care of most of the day-to-day, I found I could concentrate on what I did without too much peripheral noise, which more and more was what I felt I needed.

My biggest job of the year was to buy and sell the vehicles.

Despite our fab time in Monte Carlo with Citroen Motors, I did switch back to buying Ford Transit and Escort vans as I found them to be more reliable and held their resale price better.

The best way to do it was to buy a batch of vehicles at a time, maybe ten or fifteen depending on the age and mileage of those being replaced.

With the company running well over a hundred and fifty vehicles and each one clocking up around 50,000 miles a year, there was a high turnover.

The strategy that I found worked for me was to ask each sales representative for their very best price based on ten vehicles costing around £7k each, using finance over two years with one month paid upfront.

The clever bit was I only gave the finance house one chance to submit their bid to fund the vehicles. I would then place the business with the company that provided the best quote and would always tell the other company why they had not got the deal and by how much the other company had undercut them.

I dealt with two companies, and one representative from each.

From Lombard it was Mike, and from Barclays it was Denver.

The very first time Mike or Denver lost out on the business, they each asked if they could have another opportunity to quote as they now felt sure they could get me a better price than they had first quoted and even better than the price I had just accepted from their competitor.

'No,' I said. And that was that.

Although I was turning down the chance to get the vehicles funded at a lower price, I knew by sticking to my guns this time they would not make the same mistake again and they would in future always submit their very best price the first time. I have to say it was a strategy that worked really well and saved me a lot of time. Previously I would spend days going back and forth asking them if they could shave a bit off here or there as they had been outbid. The old way could easily take up to a week before I'd feel confident I was getting the lowest price. My new policy ensured I got the very best price on day one.

Getting the cheapest price in business is not always the best practice and not one I would follow particularly where the level of service became more important in the decision-making process. It is true that most of the time you do tend to get what you pay for. I know my own courier rates were not the cheapest in the market, but then I never set out to be the cheapest, I set out to be the best. With finance, I was just borrowing money, and as I often said to Mike and Denver, one man's pound is as good as another's.

I really liked both Denver and Mike but never socialised with either of them at the time. It was a rule I had about mixing business with pleasure, so I was unaware and, as it transpired so were they, that they both lived in the same village.

And this small world just gets smaller, and smaller, and smaller.

# Chapter Thirty-one

For many years now I have supported a donkey charity based out in Israel called Lucy's UK Donkey Foundation. Although most of the work they do is based in Israel, it is a UK registered charity, and the work Lucy and her small team undertake with donkeys is genuinely incredible. If anyone asked me who my heroine was, I always said, without hesitation, Lucy.

It all started back in the early nineties when Lucy left the UK to volunteer on an Israeli kibbutz. Being a devoted animal lover, after her first year in Israel she found her way to Jerusalem, where she ended up volunteering the next five years of her life at the Jerusalem Society for the Prevention of Cruelty to Animals (JSPCA).

She began to volunteer there seven days a week and became chief keeper of the cattery. It was during this time she came across her beloved Donk, a wonderful donkey character who belonged to a Bedouin man. Donk was often hobbled outside the SPCA – hobbling is a practice used to tether one leg to a post, or, in Donk's case, both front legs together so they can't wander off. Sometimes rope is used, but more often than not, in Israel and Palestine, rough string and even wire is chosen. This practice is banned in the UK, but out there in the nineties it was widely used, and still is today.

Poor Donk's legs were bleeding and torn, but with Lucy's tender care and devotion he soon recovered. Realising the donkey was getting medical care for free, his owner would take him to her for what he called refuelling, sometimes leaving him with her for months on end.

This went on for a few years until Lucy managed to raise enough money to buy Donk. The bargaining over the price for Donk was ridiculous, and

Lucy paid well over the top for him, knowing the owner could probably go off and purchase another two donkeys with the sum. But Lucy didn't care. She had her Donk.

She wasn't stupid. She knew Donk would be the first of many rescues, because so many donkeys were suffering with malnutrition, sores, overgrown feet, lacerations, fleas, worms, dehydration and worse. So when her time in Israel came to an end, having witnessed these all-too-frequent horrors, Lucy vowed that one day she would return and start a sanctuary for donkeys.

At the time Lucy was working as a flight attendant, and Donk was flown over to the UK, where he received much publicity. This really helped Lucy in her mission to set up a charity, register it in the UK and fundraise for her to return to Israel and embark upon her mission to help many more donkeys. Tragically, Donk passed away one year after arriving in the UK, but he certainly left a legacy.

Lucy now cares for over one hundred donkeys and lives in Israel full-time with her husband Adi and their son Robert, or as I like to call them, my big and little brothers.

It really is tough for her out there. Life is hard and the work she does is incredible. I have seen for myself first-hand the condition some of these donkeys are in when they get rescued. I honestly don't know how she does it. I guess it must be something to do with seeing the pain in the donkey's eyes when they first get rescued to how changed they become after just a few weeks in Lucy's care. That must be so rewarding. What really struck me when I visited was how gentle the donkeys are around people. You would think knowing how they have been treated there would be at least some aggression and lack of trust, but I can assure you there never is. Truly remarkable, no other way to put it.

The charity also provides an outreach programme visiting villages. She takes a qualified vet along with her who does his work at cost, and between them they not only dispense medicines but also educate the owners on better ways to take care of the animals. It's certainly an uphill struggle, that's for sure.

When asked what she would like her legacy to be, Lucy says that all she really wants is for ignorance and cruelty towards animals to stop. For those people whom she has strived to change, to have them learn that there is another way. That animals are sentient beings who give their lives to serve their owners and work so hard, and the fact that, in return, they deserve at the very least a gentle hand and to have their basic needs met. And of course for donkeys and all animals to be treated more humanely, the world over, in memory of her Donk, and for all the hardship, toil and lost little lives along the way not to have been in vain.

It was while serving as a trustee for the donkey charity that I met with Ann Widdecombe. She, along with Uri Geller, were both patrons of Lucy's charity, and I wanted to see if I could persuade her to do some publicity to raise awareness of the cause.

I phoned her office and spoke to her secretary, who set up a meeting with her at the House of Commons.

The day duly arrived and I drove down to London, slightly apprehensive but also excited. This was going to be a great opportunity to meet her and have a sneaky look around Westminster.

Once through the usual security measures, I was shown into the central lobby and asked to wait. I was told Ann's secretary would come down to meet me and take me to Ann's office. After a short while I saw Ann herself coming down some stairs. She made her way to security, who pointed my way. Then she made a beeline towards me.

As she approached, she stretched out her hand to shake mine and said in her brisk no-nonsense fashion, 'Hello, have you won me in a raffle?'

Flummoxed, I stammered, 'Err, what? I mean, pardon?'

'Have you won me in a raffle? Is that why you're here, to have afternoon tea with me? They're always raffling me off for that.' She continued without pausing for breath. 'My secretary is off today, you see.'

'Oh right, I see. Well no. Actually, I'm never very good at raffles, I never seem to win. I'm here from Lucy's donkey charity. I'm here to chat about possible publicity opportunities you might be able to help with.'

Roaring so anyone within twenty feet could hear, she said, 'Oh you're the donkey man!'

'I've been called a few things in my time, Ann,' I said with a grin.

She has a wicked sense of humour and a rather naughty laugh, both of which were on full display.

Ice broken, she apologised for not remembering why I was there and suggested that as I was here anyway, and she had already reserved a table, we should talk over some afternoon tea in the Members' Dining Room, which she assured me was always very good.

'Follow me,' she commanded, and with that she was off. It was hard to keep up with her. She might be a small woman but she can walk at one hell of a pace.

We went through some large double doors, down a long wood panel corridor with Ann always a few steps ahead of me saying 'hello' and nodding to various people we passed on our way to the restaurant.

On entering, Ann was greeted by the maître d' and immediately escorted to the table that had been reserved for her and one guest. I took a moment to take in the room, which was large, impressive and adorned with beautiful flock wallpaper, wooden ornate ceilings and antique paintings on every wall. This was without doubt the most spectacular dining room I have ever been in.

However, it soon became apparent it was going to be nigh-on impossible to have any sort of sensible conversation with her. As soon as we had sat down, numerous people, some I recognised as other MPs, barged over to the table and without any apology simply started talking over us.

'Will you be voting today, Ann?' one of them asked.

'Are you going to that meeting tonight?' said another.

It was one interruption after another. Clearly the business of Parliament was far more important than any business I might have had with her. Perhaps they too also thought I had won tea with her in a raffle.

Although Ann was very pleasant, and the afternoon tea was superb, I regret that I really got nowhere discussing any of my promotional ideas before my time was up and I was being escorted back to the central lobby and out the door.

Unperturbed, I tried my luck with the other half of the dream team, Uri Geller, and had much more success.

He agreed to do a small publicity shoot at his house down south on the banks of the Thames.

Between us, we arranged for a donkey from a local farm to come to his house for a photo shoot.

Uri is a fascinating guy, and he spent a lot of time telling stories of the numerous celebrities he had met over the years. He even showed us his custom-built 1976 Cadillac car emblazoned with two thousand pieces of twisted and contorted cutlery signed by some of the most famous people in the world, and all of it had been painstakingly riveted to the car's body.

I was dying to see him bend a spoon but didn't have the courage to ask. Thankfully, one member of the press did, and of course he agreed. Turning, he asked his wife to fetch some spoons from the house, and when she returned she handed them to him. I guess these must have been bought for the job and not their everyday dinner service, that or they'd always be running out. 'Pudding, darling? Where are the spoons— oh not again!'

I watched him like a hawk. Was he going to bend it with some force when we were distracted?

Far from it. From what I could see anyway.

He carried on talking to us about this and that while he rubbed the side of a spoon. He wasn't even paying any attention to the spoon and right in front of my eyes it started to bend. I couldn't believe what I was seeing. There was clearly no force being used, he was just gently rubbing his fingers on the neck of the spoon, yet it was bending.

He stopped and looked at it as if in shock himself. 'Oh look, that's already bent. Who would like it?' And he handed it to the man from the press who had asked him for a demonstration.

Six spoons later, and five happy members of the press, along with me, all had a bent spoon in our hands.

Promo pictures with Uri and the donkey done, Uri agreed to sign my spoon and I promised I would raffle it at an auction in aid of Lucy's charity.

About twelve months later I did. I was excited to see how much it would fetch and who would buy it. For the bargain sum of £250 it was bought by my local MP. Handing it over, I said, 'Can I offer you as a prize in the raffle too?'

Bemused, he said, 'Why would you want to do that?'

Oh well, maybe it's only Ann Widdecombe that does that.

www.lucysdonkeyfoundation.org.uk

* * *

What follows is a conversation between me and my editor.

Editor: I love this chapter Nick, I remember being wowed by Uri Geller bending spoons. However, I can't find any mention of either Uri Geller or Ann Widdecombe on Lucy's website.

Me: Well in 2015 Lucy's service with the original charity she founded ended and she went on to help establish a new charity in order to continue her own mission independently.

Editor: Okay. So just to be clear, the donkey charity where Uri and Ann were involved is not the same as the charity Lucy runs now. Is that correct?

Me: Yes that's right, to be very transparent - Ann Widdecombe and Uri Geller are not affiliated in any way with her new charity - lucysdonkeyfoundation.org.uk

Editor: I think we need to make that clear.

Me: Really?

Editor: Unless you want to be sued.

Me: Eeeerrrrrrr, okkkkkkkkkkkay. How do I do that?

Editor: I'm not the writer Nick. That's your job.

Me: Um. Oh sod it, how about if I just put this conversation at the end of the chapter?

Editor: As long as you make me sound very intelligent, attractive and professional. By the way, I'm reading Proust at the moment, in French. Just so you know.

Me: Lol, you know I'm going to put that in now, don't you!

# Chapter Thirty-two

With the business growing steadily and the management team also expanding, I was starting to get away more often so decided it might be nice to sell my apartment in Spain and get a villa. The idea of having my own pool was the key attraction for me. It was far better than sharing the communal pool, not that the pool at Puebla Aida ever got that busy.

The search began to find my dream villa. I drove up and down the coast covering many miles for six months. I ended up buying a brand-new villa on Calle Valencia that was less than a quarter of a mile away from my apartment at Puebla Aida. I had seen the plot, then watched the villa start being constructed. I had done my homework and knew this was the one for me.

I had been to see the villa a few times, which was now about three-quarters built. Firstly with the developer Feliciano and his sales girl Maria, but then I snuck back late at night alone when the construction men had left the site. I could fantasise about it one day being mine.

I had been back in the UK for a few days, and having mulled it over, and more importantly ensured I could raise the money, I telephoned the Spanish sales office to make an offer. I reminded Maria that I had seen the villa the previous week, and she remembered me.

When I made my offer, which was about ten per cent below the asking price, Maria said she would check it out with Feliciano and ring me back. Based on what the other villas had recently sold for, she was not optimistic my offer would be accepted. The following day she called me back to confirm the answer was no, Feliciano wanted the full asking price. I decided to leave it for a week and see if they would call me back.

I was the first to blink, and the following week I called again and said, 'Okay, I'll give you the full asking price.'

'Oh, but it's gone up in price now,' came the reply from a sheepish Maria. 'I'll need to check with Feliciano again.'

I threw a tantrum after I heard that news, but once I had put my toys back in my pram I realised I was being hasty. I knew, even at the new figure, it was still a good deal. Four weeks passed and I was about to ring again when I received a call from Maria. 'It's just a courtesy call,' she said, explaining that the villa I was interested in was about to go up again in price.

'Okay, you win,' I said. 'I'll pay the asking price before Feliciano increases it again, but please tell him this is not how negotiations are meant to work.' Sale and demand at work I suppose. We became good friends after that.

I had to wait another three months before the villa was finished. This gave me time to sell my penthouse, which I managed to sell for the full asking price. I had actually made a nice little profit. It was clear that property prices in Spain, certainly on the Costa del Sol, were experiencing a boom. Jose acted for me again both on the sale and on the new villa.

I contacted Elona and asked if she would come and furnish my new home – interior designers really have that knack for making things look good.

Despite all my best efforts, my forty-third birthday was still fast approaching. It's so annoying how birthdays do that.

I had been running my company since I was seventeen. Apart from a brief spell as a self-employed motorcycle courier, this had been my only job. So what's that… twenty-six years as a boss. Twenty-six years with the stress and responsibility of the lives of my staff and the expectations of my customers plonked squarely on my shoulders.

Twenty-six years of making life-changing decisions every day.

Twenty-six years of negotiating.

Twenty-six years of hustling.

Twenty-six years of stress.

I knew one day I'd look back with pride and a sense of pleasure, but right now I was too immersed, like diving underwater in a swimming pool;

you know there's life outside of it, but you can't see, hear, smell or touch it. All you can feel is the water surrounding you.

It felt like I'd dragged the company all the way from when I was a boy with a motorbike and a dream working from my tiny bedroom at Dad's terrace house in 1977, to now, employing me as the managing director, two further directors, a sales director, finance director, general manager, human resources manager, sales manager, three branch managers and their deputies. There was also a night manager (Birmingham) plus 165 full-time drivers and a small number of part-time staff. Also, to support this team there were two additional members of staff working in the accounts department and a central operations room in Birmingham, with four operators who looked after some of the larger contracts. We even had our own in-house repair centre employing three engineers so we could repair any faulty Blockbuster hardware. Last but not least, my wonderful PA Eileen and before her Tanya, who had both helped keep me in check, protecting me from unsolicited sales calls but most importantly ensuring that I could take my twenty-minute power nap every afternoon, something I do even today.

By the end of 2002, I was employing a total of 188 full-time staff.

The HQ was still in Birmingham and this was being manned twenty-four hours a day seven days a week. We didn't even close on Christmas Day.

The company was now operating from three main offices in Birmingham, Warrington and Cambridge, and we had control of a further six store locations dotted around the UK. Around twenty-five of our full-time drivers were home-based, scattered all over the country; something that was way ahead of its time. These strategically placed storerooms and home-based drivers ensured we could reach almost any part of the UK within an hour.

The business was extremely profitable, with no bad debt and a healthy bank balance. The company had no borrowings, other than the finance for the fleet of vehicles, and we had numerous contracts that were with an impressive list of blue-chip companies.

From little acorns whopping great big companies grow.

And I was shattered.

I felt like the energy and drive I had in the early years was gone.

Up until the previous two years, I'd loved it. But now I was struggling. I was burnt-out.

Frazzled.

It was early November 2002 and the phone on my desk buzzed with an internal call.

Eileen, my PA said, 'It's him again. On the phone asking for you. The one who won't tell me where he's from or what it's about.'

He'd called a couple of times. Probably a sales call, so I'd given her the standard, 'Tell him I'm in a meeting, please,' line.

Chances are, I probably would have been in a meeting because that's how most of my days were spent, having meetings with various heads of departments and being brought up to speed with what was happening. Gone were the days when I was the entrepreneur meeting with prospective clients, answering the phones, interviewing drivers, running the accounts department, designing new sales brochures, or even carrying out some of the deliveries. No, those days were long, and sadly, gone.

But this guy was nothing if not persistent. It was late on a Friday afternoon and I was curious, so I told her to put him through.

'Mr Terry, thank you for taking my call.' His voice was deep and rich, like that of an actor. He went on to explain he was a corporate headhunter.

I didn't say it out loud, but I thought, what the heck is that?

He said that he represented a very large company that had been watching BXT for the past twelve months, and they wanted to know if I would be interested in selling.

My internal Homer Simpson staring at a stack of doughnuts woke up. Mmmmmmm.

He explained that he was not at liberty to divulge who the company he represented was, but he assured me I'd be familiar with the name.

Of course I was curious. And excited. And... hopeful, I think.

Arranging to meet on Monday, we picked a location well away from the offices, as the last thing I wanted was anyone within BXT to know I was even considering selling my business, not even my co-directors at this stage.

The weekend dragged. The meeting did not.

We sat and chatted over coffee, outlining how his clients had approached him and roughly what their expectations were. It came across as a very sensible situation.

It was also the right time. Boy oh boy, if it came off, was it the right time.

By Friday of the same week, he was able to confirm that he had reported back to his client that I would tentatively be happy to meet with them to explore the possibility of a sale. He was authorised to inform me of the company he was working for. It was Business Post plc, and their CEO Paul was looking forward to meeting me.

I knew a little about Business Post, but by the time I met with Paul, I knew a lot more. A great saying in life is 'Fail to prepare, prepare to fail', a motto I still hold true today. I had spent the last few days doing my homework and I was now ready for our initial meeting.

The company was impressive, listed on the FTSE 100, employing 2,000 staff with a turnover of some £200 million.

Over the course of a few weeks we had more than a dozen meetings at their impressive offices, the culmination of which was that we agreed a six-figure price for the acquisition of BXT, one that Paul felt was too high and I felt was too low. In hindsight, it was probably about right.

In deals such as these, the small print matters. In my case I wasn't to get all the money up front, but rather I was offered eighty per cent with a final twenty per cent earn-out based on meeting two criteria.

The first was to secure a new twelve-month contract with Blockbuster Video. Following the due diligence process, which took about five weeks, Business Post's team had identified only one real weakness in the deal. It was the fact that the contract we had with Blockbuster, which at that time represented around fifteen per cent of my company's turnover, was coming to an end. Their recommendation to Business Post was to be sure a new contract was in place before handing over ten per cent of the purchase price.

The final ten per cent withheld would not be paid unless the company achieved a turnover in line with last year's accounts and a net profit equal to, or more than, the previous year. For every pound under the previous year's net profit, Business Post would retain five pounds. Sadly, for me, the contract did not work the other way.

There was a risk to it, but one I was prepared to take, and although I could not do much about the clause on turnover and profit, I could certainly have some control and influence over the new Blockbuster contract.

Sir, I have a cunning plan.

Is it as cunning as…

Oh yes!

Swiftly arranging a meeting with Jason, the director at Blockbuster, I confided in him I was about to sell BXT. I even told him who was acquiring my company. I then reminded him that the contract we had to supply services was soon coming to an end. I suggested that if we could agree on new terms now, while I was still in total control, it might be beneficial for both of us.

New terms were outlined and agreed in principle at that meeting and I promised he would be getting a written contract confirming these new arrangements within the next few days. I wanted to first run it by Paul for his approval.

The day I went to see Paul he was extremely busy and could only spare me a few minutes. I briefly explained that I had tentatively agreed on new terms with Blockbuster, but before signing off I wanted to be sure Paul was happy with them.

I am convinced at this point he had simply forgotten that the renewal of this contract affected the release of ten per cent of the purchase price. He just took a very brief look at the terms and told me it all looked fine.

Later that day I sent Paul an email thanking him for agreeing to the terms for the Blockbuster contract, and it had now been signed off.

From my very first meeting to agreeing the sale, the whole process had only taken three months. My directors were informed after the first month, and all staff were advised in the second month. Detailed due diligence was carried out by the Business Post acquisitions team in month three, and the sale of BXT was to take place on 28th February 2003.

Arrangements had been made for all parties to meet at the offices of Business Post's lawyers. I sat on one side of a very large table with my lawyer, a lovely guy called David Beach, while Paul, his finance director, PA and a team of four lawyers all sat on the opposite side. Seven against two.

There were numerous legal papers to be signed and my lawyer simply suggested that if I trusted him, I should just allow him to sign all the papers on my behalf without the need for me to check each and every page, as he had already read through them. I trusted him, and apart from the final page requiring my signature, this is what we did.

Just before I signed off the very last page, my lawyer asked to see the cheque that Business Post's lawyers had pre-prepared.

The amount was wrong and my lawyer pointed out they were exactly ten per cent light of the amount agreed in the contract.

The lead lawyer, a pompous man, started to explain that twenty per cent was being held back on retention as final payments were subject to certain conditions being met. He even went on to explain that ten per cent retention was related to turnover and profit targets needing to be met and the final ten per cent on the renewal of the Blockbuster contract.

As if I needed to be told this.

My lawyer turned to look at me and I couldn't help smiling.

'Didn't you agree and sign off a new twelve-month contract with Blockbuster a few weeks ago?' he said.

'Yes,' I said, nodding.

'Well, we were not aware of this,' came the abrupt reply from the legal beagles on the other side.

Au contraire! Not only had we brought along a copy of the newly signed Blockbuster contract, but we accompanied it with a copy of my email that I had sent to Paul thanking him for confirming he was happy with the new terms agreed with Blockbuster.

Red faces all round on the opposite side of the table.

The Business Post team left the room for what was clearly going to be an interesting conversation between themselves, and about half an hour later they returned with a second cheque in hand. My lawyer confirmed I was good to sign the last page.

With a stroke of a pen, BXT had been sold.

I'm not really sure what I was expecting, maybe a fanfare of some kind. This was after all a momentous moment for me, and a very proud one too. I had achieved everything I set out to do as a seventeen-year-old.

Before leaving my house that morning my girlfriend had given me a lovely engraved pen which she said I was to use when signing the sale contract. It was a silver pen manufactured by Cross pen makers and engraved with my initials, NDT. It was a lovely, thoughtful gift.

Once Paul had countersigned the final page of our agreement, he too presented me with the pen that he had used, also a nice touch.

Both pens were identical. Same make and model, the only difference was mine had my initials on the side and Paul's had the Business Post logo. Both pens sit side by side on my bookshelf in my home office. What are the odds?

Some things you just can't make up.

One more for the book, Dad.

# Chapter Thirty-three

They say be careful of what you wish for, and there's some truth to that. For the past two years I'd been running on empty. I was washed out. The company had stripped me of every ounce of energy I had. So I sold it. It was the right thing to do. On many levels.

The night I signed for Business Post to take it off my hands, I drove home, the two pens visible on the seat next to me; one engraved with my initials, a gift from my girlfriend, and the other handed to me by the CEO of Business Post following his signature on the same document.

I kept glancing at them, as if I needed reminding of what I'd just done.

When I reached home I stripped off my suit and took a shower before riffling through the wardrobe for something to wear that didn't involve choosing an accompanying tie.

In the kitchen I found a card propped up against a bottle of champagne. Nice touch. I smiled at the card from my girlfriend and popped the bubbles, pouring a glass and taking out the cheque I'd been handed in exchange for my company. I stared at the six zeroes and the number before it.

I'd done it.

I'd fucking well done it.

I was a fucking multimillionaire.

A shiver snaked down my spine.

Lifting the glass I took a sip, then raised it and said quietly, 'BXT.' I've never admitted this to anyone, but I cried. Not sobs, just tears. I don't even know why. I'd got what I wanted, and I'd done it the hard way. I was a smidge over forty, retired, and I'd never have to worry about money again.

I was contracted to stay on for twelve months, but was only required to work ten days a month in the first six months, and then just five days a month in the last six months. The only stipulation was, one of the days that I attended had to be for the monthly board meeting.

During my last six months I used to call Paul's personal assistant at the beginning of every month, a lovely lady called Barbara, and I would ask her what date was in the diary for the next board meeting. I would then ensure I worked the two days before and two days after, thus completing my contracted days within a week.

Mark, the sales director, had been promoted to MD, leaving my role simply to act as a consultant and to try and ensure a smooth transition.

The first six months of the year went extremely well, and barring any major disaster, BXT was easily going to hit the financial targets set. Sure enough, by month ten, these had already been achieved with two months still to go. The board were delighted.

The final payment, the last ten per cent owed to me, was released to me some six months later. The delay was simply because Business Post had to get the accounts independently verified, which was fair enough.

My last official day at BXT was to be the twenty-eighth of February 2004, but as I'd worked all the days I was required to do, I secretly decided my last day in the office would be Friday the twentieth.

I called Paul around midday and explained I had now completed my contract, worked all the days required and was leaving tonight. Paul had assumed I would be going on the last day of the month, as had everyone else, so my news came as a bit of a surprise. He wished me well and promised that he would get in touch to arrange a proper farewell dinner.

At around five that afternoon, aware my general manager Terry was about to leave his office to enjoy the weekend, I knocked on his door, entered, and closed it behind me. Terry had been with the company through good times and bad and was one of my longest-serving members of staff. He had started with me some eighteen years previously, joining the company first as a driver before being promoted to branch manager at the Coventry branch. I closed that branch during the hard recession in the late eighties and he became the branch manager at Birmingham. Eventually, he was promoted to general manager with numerous responsibilities, including overseeing the day-to-day running of all branches.

I quietly explained that today was my last day and, of course, he was shocked. I think he had been secretly arranging a farewell surprise party, but clearly with my departure tonight this was not going to happen.

I asked him not to say anything to the others when he left that night. I wanted to speak to a few people individually. With that, he stood up, shook my hand, and we said our goodbyes. I found it all rather emotional, but then I knew I would.

Then I had a very similar conversation with my sales manager Jim, before chatting to Matt, my branch manager. Both appeared to be shocked that I was leaving today. It was the only way I could handle the situation; no fuss, just quietly saying goodbye and leaving.

Mark, who was now the new managing director, was next. He too was a little surprised but wished me well, and we agreed to keep in touch. We had come a long way from that encounter in the Chinese restaurant.

Finally, I went into the accounts department, where my finance director, Veronica, was still hard at work, although about to get ready to leave for home. Veronica had worked for me for as long as Terry, and she was, like all my key members of staff, wonderful and loyal.

Hopefully, in return, I had been a good boss. I have since been told that I was seen by most as being firm but fair – I'll settle for that.

I think more than anyone else Veronica had become aware that I was tired of running the company, both physically and mentally, and deep down I think she was pleased for me. She had played a pivotal role in my life and I was truly sorry to be saying goodbye to her.

When I had said goodbye to the other members of staff I had tried to hold myself in check and not become too emotional. Veronica of course saw straight through me and immediately hugged me.

I broke down. I couldn't help it.

Twenty-six years of my life and it had come to this, me sneaking off so no one could make a fuss. Veronica understood, and I will forever be grateful for her help, kindness, and support.

We hugged again, I composed myself the best I could and I walked out of BXT for the very last time. That walk out, head held high, footsteps confident, was possibly the most difficult thing I have ever done.

Two months later, Paul Carvell was true to his word and kindly arranged a farewell dinner where we had a splendid meal at the Hotel du Vin in Birmingham.

Mark and Veronica stayed with BXT for another twelve months but found the new regime difficult to work under. Paul had left Business Post and the new CEO did not have the same vision as Paul had for BXT. I always remember him telling me, and my staff, that his intention was only to develop and expand the business, especially its specialised added value services. Jobs were safe, there would be no redundancies and everyone could look forward to a secure future. His favourite saying was, 'I will only have a gentle hand on the tiller.' It was a memorable saying and sentiment, but one he was unable to deliver.

Under the new regime of Business Post plc, all BXT's offices were soon closed down and amalgamated into their company's own branch offices. Managers and drivers were let go or decided to leave of their own accord; better to jump than be pushed I heard one say. Most contracts were lost; even the Blockbuster contract was moved twelve months later to another firm, although that might have been a blessing in disguise, as not long afterwards they disappeared off the high street altogether. Technology was moving at such a fast pace, collecting a video or DVD from a rental shop was becoming old school. Downloading or watching the latest films from the likes of Netflix and Amazon was the future.

It was such a shame to hear that within two years of selling my company, a company that had taken me twenty-six years of blood, sweat and more than a few tears to build up, it was gone forever.

Everything changes. Everything evolves and moves on. As hard as it seems, we must too. Life's too short for regrets; just ask my brother Paul.

I have lovely memories; some I laugh at, some I shake my head at. They all mean something to me. They're all special. But life goes on. One day you're suited and booted sitting in your office, and the next you're at home. That's how life rocks.

Oh, you know, and it does take the edge off it when you're young and a millionaire. I might be a bit sad for a while, but I'm not bloody stupid.

# Chapter Thirty-four

So what's a man to do after retirement? Well, there's always Spain.
I love the sun. I love the culture in Spain, the food and the wine. I
also love the siestas; even at the height of BXT, when (organised) chaos
ruled the day, I still found time for a power nap. To be successful you've
got to know your body, fuel it well with good food and regular exercise.
Your body and your mind are your weapons. They are what makes the
difference between you and your competitors in business. Disrespect your
body and your mind, abuse them, and they won't function properly. When
that happens, you've lost your edge. Lose the edge, and you've lost the
game. Your competitors win. I recognised right from the start that my body
functioned much better with a power nap halfway through the day. Yes I
could have fought it, battled through with strong coffee and an iron will,
but I didn't. I recognised that's what my body needed and embraced it.
Doing that made me sharper. Sharper than my competitors. I won.

The Spanish understand this, and I love the fact that everything shuts
down for a power nap halfway through the day. That's my kind of place.

I knew I was exhausted, but it wasn't until the sale of BXT went through
and I had some time on my hands that I fully recognised just how shattered
I was. I was bone weary, the kind of exhaustion a few good sleeps can't fix;
I needed recuperation.

Up until then the breaks I'd enjoyed in Spain had been fleeting: a day
here, two days there. All lovely, but rushed. To recover, I needed more. A
lot more. So I moved out there for a proper length of time, which was just
what the doctor ordered.

Daytimes I'd doss and chill, maybe take in a nice lunch somewhere or a
trip to the market, but if I was going out in the evenings, I tended to head

down the coast to Marbella or Puerto Banús. I have never been one for nightlife and clubbing, but when on holiday you have to experience the vibe, and it was certainly found in that neck of the woods.

Never one to completely sit idly by, I decided to look for a new place out there, ideally closer to Marbella. The first development I looked at was of course White Pearl Beach, which had been completed some years ago. I was very interested to see whether the apartments at the front with the sea view that I was assured 'cannot ever be built on, Mr Terry' still had a sea view.

They didn't. They now had a five-storey block of apartments built in front of them. So much for the sea view.

Driving down the coast road about half a mile before the exit to Marbella at Los Monteros, I noticed a sign saying 'Luxury Apartments For Sale'. Underneath in big lettering it read, 'Show Apartment Open'. It reminded me very much of all those years ago when I had seen a sign in Harborne for the Yew Tree developments. It was a déjà vu moment.

The sales office for Los Monteros Playa was on the ground floor within one of the apartments. The complex was in a quiet and exclusive residential area of Reserva de Los Monteros. It was a gated community with twenty-four-hour security and a perimeter camera video system. Think Fort Knox but more discreet. All these front-line deluxe apartments had great sea views and direct access to the beach. I also knew from my time spent in Spain that some of the best beaches can be found in this area.

The gardens were already mature thanks to planting over fifty fully grown palm trees. It was beautifully landscaped with lakes, streams, and swimming pools. This was a different world from what I had been used to.

I was told that the apartment on the first floor above the sales office was still available and, according to the salesgirl, it was probably one of the best in terms of its location and views.

After a brief walk around the apartment, I knew instantly that again this had my name written all over it. I returned downstairs via the marble staircase to the sales office and asked, 'How much is it, please?'

Okay, I now needed a large sangria. I couldn't really justify spending that sort of money on what was after all just a three-bedroom apartment. Every bedroom had its own en suite. The master bedroom had one of the biggest fitted-out dressing rooms I have ever seen. The lounge alone was twice the size of the whole of my apartment at Puebla Aida, and the kitchen had every appliance, including a large American fridge-freezer with an ice dispenser. The private underground secure garage that came with this apartment had spaces for four cars, but it was pricey.

I called my lawyer Jose, who had now become my friend. I think it was when he said it was bound to go up in price over the next five years that I was convinced. I needed to invest part of the money from the sale of BXT into something, why not a luxury property?

I checked with a local estate agent what my villa on Mijas golf course would be worth. I was pleasantly surprised to find that in the three years I had owned the villa it had gone up in value, so perhaps this apartment might be affordable after all.

For a change, I didn't jump straight in but instead took a whole twenty-four hours to think it through. Returning the following day and managing to negotiate a small discount, I handed over a cheque with my ten per cent non-refundable deposit. I was about to live in high-end Marbella. I'd come a long way from the little terrace house in Harborne.

My first visitor was Elona, my interior designer, who I asked to furnish my new apartment and asked out to dinner. I'd asked her a few times and she always kissed me on the cheek and said no. Oh well, no harm in trying.

'The rooms are massive,' she said, standing in the middle of the voluminous lounge and spinning around in circles. 'It's going to be expensive.'

When is it not?

We agreed a budget that made my knees go weak and my hand itch for another strong sangria, and yet again she did a fabulous job.

The entire project had cost a lot, which was fine. It was an investment. What I hadn't anticipated was how much it would cost to maintain the property. There was the community charge, to cover the costs for the general running of the complex. At the start, this annual service charge was six thousand euros per year. Within eight years it would double.

On top of that I had to fork out four thousand euros in council tax, called IBI in Spain. Once I added in the cost of insurance, heating, water, telephone, TV services and cleaning, etc., it was costing me around twenty thousand euros per year. I found it hard to justify this, but the final nail in the coffin was that, following a new government directive, the large swimming pool that my apartment overlooked had to employ a lifeguard or be fenced off and closed.

The housing committee had voted for a lifeguard only to be present between the months of July and September; these were the months I tended to remain in the UK. I was devastated. The fence they erected around the pool to stop owners from using it was ugly. The fact I couldn't use it was unacceptable. It was time to move on.

I placed the property on the market and was lucky to find a buyer within three months. The apartment was sold fully furnished and I made a tidy profit.

After selling, I realised I had now owned property in Spain for more than seventeen years. I thought I needed to take a step back and consider my options. Maybe look to buy a property in another country, or just invest the money in the UK property market. Time to hit the pause button.

I always booked flights well in advance, often at least twelve months ahead, so although I no longer had a property in Spain, I still had flights booked. I decided to take most of these flights and just rent a villa or apartment for my stay.

Renting a lock-up for all my clothes and personal items meant I could travel light with only hand baggage. I still had my car in Spain, so transport was never going to be an issue.

However, I missed having my own pad. Renting's okay, but it's never quite like they portray in the adverts, and it doesn't have the same feel as when it's yours.

I thought about trying somewhere different, America maybe? Or perhaps Turkey? But Spain felt like it was in my blood. So on the next trip, I determined to find a small place to buy as a stopgap until something perfect came up, just so I had a base of my own out there.

During these latter trips, I'd started renting from a chap called Dawson. He had a few properties along the coast, and they were always clean and comfortable.

On a mission, I scoured the local property magazines, spending days driving round looking in numerous estate agent's windows, but nothing jumped out.

Location was important; isn't it always? I wanted somewhere between Marbella and Fuengirola, as it's nice and close to Malaga Airport. I don't mind driving and have a good sense of direction, but it just makes the journey harder.

Having no luck finding anything in the first few days, I picked up the latest edition of Hot Properties magazine, a monthly publication from Viva Estates. Inside they were advertising a furnished two-bedroom apartment for sale in Calahonda. I wasn't overkeen on Calahonda, but the property looked rather nice for the money, and anyway, this was only going to be a stopgap.

I headed to the nearest Viva office, which was in La Cala, only to be told that property was now sold, but she did have another one that might suit my requirements that had just come on the market. It was so hot off the press she didn't have any sale particulars, but what she did have was far better, a set of keys.

After I checked that I had time, the agent offered to take me to see it straight away. As soon as I walked in I loved it and made an offer on the spot.

Once back at the office, the agent put the offer forward, which was accepted.

Woo-hoo, I was back on the Española property ladder.

'Mm, hum. Yep, they're still here,' the agent said into the phone, still on the line to the owner. 'You will? Oh that's great. Ten minutes, yes. Okay, see you then.'

Apparently he was on his way to the office in order that we could complete the paperwork there and then. Property transactions are so civilised out there.

As we waited for the vendor to arrive, the agent peered through the window and said, 'Oh, here he is now!'

Who walks in? Dawson, the man I'd been renting from and chatting to for all these months.

'You!' he said, pointing and laughing.

'You!' I responded, doing the same.

'You know each other?' the agent said, bemused.

'My best customer just got better,' Dawson said. 'Where do I sign?'

# Chapter Thirty-five

I sold my business on 28th February 2003. Since then a few people have approached me with various business ideas asking if I would be interested in joining them. All but two I turned down.

Then there was Denver.

Me and Denver go way back to a time when I was financing a fleet of vans every year and Denver would bid for the business. At the time we didn't socialise, as it's always tricky mixing work with pleasure. Once I retired, we became good mates.

'I've got a great idea,' Denver exclaimed.

This, I thought, will either be messy or expensive, and quite possibly both.

'Go on,' I encouraged him.

'It's a business venture.' Yep, my thoughts were correct. Both of them. 'Can I run it by you, see what you think?'

Why not.

We met later that week, and clearly Denver had been a busy boy. Friends or not, if you're going to pitch a business, pitch it. Don't fanny around with back of fag packet presentations or bullet points scrawled on an old envelope, and Denver knew this. His presentation was slick, concise and thorough.

The year was 2006. Italy was staking its claim at the World Cup, Saddam Hussain had been found and killed, and artificial grass, or AstroTurf, was an 'Oooh, you can do that?' phenomenon yet to hit.

Denver said, 'Very few people have even heard of it, but if you think about it, it's a no-brainer. I remember you always telling me you hated cutting the grass.'

That was true.

'If you could have had artificial grass back then that looked just like the real thing but needed no maintenance, would you have gone for it?'

'Without a doubt.'

Spreading his arms out wide he said, 'There you go.'

He had a good point. Plus I liked him, liked his style, his work ethic and his attitude. And I needed a new challenge. BUT. But, but, but. Really, was there really a business to be made out of it?

Artificial lawns have come a long way over the years, and you can not only see them in many gardens, but the council have started using them at the side of roads and highways. Schools have them, sports arenas and leisure centres, and even old people's care homes. Every good DIY outlet is selling lawns, and only recently I saw a lawn being sold in a plumber's merchants.

But back when Denver suggested the concept to me he was ahead of his time. Only a handful of companies could be found selling this product and even less actually installing it.

Posing as a potential customer, Denver had made some inquiries and managed to secure a viewing at a property where they had recently laid a lawn in a front garden for him to see the end result.

At this stage I was still not convinced. I could see it had some merit but I had always thought of artificial lawn as being very plastic and hard. To this day I can vividly recall my grandma's artificial plastic roses which she proudly displayed in her lounge next to the TV I rented to her, and you could tell they were plastic from twenty feet away. Plastic lawns had a similar feeling to me, although Denver assured me that things had moved on in recent years and it was now much better.

I agreed to drive to Buxton where this lawn had been laid to see it for myself. Having been given the address by Denver, we agreed to meet at the property the following Sunday morning. He went in his car, as he lived over in Fradley and he was already over halfway there compared to me, travelling up from Worcestershire.

I arrived at the end of the street five minutes before the agreed time of 10am and was pleased to see I had still not lost my skills as an on-time courier. I called Denver's mobile and he told me he was still ten minutes away but went on to say that the company had called him on Saturday and explained that the people who lived at the house had gone away for the weekend so we were just to let ourselves into their front garden. Denver suggested, as I was already in the street, I make my way to the house and he would meet me there.

I found what I thought was the right house, got out of my car and walked over to the little front gate. I peered over the gate and looked at the front lawn, then I stepped through the gate and took a closer look. I stood on the lawn. I even got down on my hands and knees, and only then did I realise I must be at the wrong house because this was real grass. I made a quick exit out of the garden because I thought I was at the wrong house and was worried that the owner might challenge me about what I was doing in his front garden. I got back into my car and called Denver. 'It's the wrong house number, mate,' I said. 'That house has a real lawn.'

Two minutes later Denver's car pulled up behind mine and we both got out of our cars and I again repeated, 'We are at the wrong house.'

'Can't be,' he said, double-checking the address he'd been given. 'Let's have a look.'

Together we walked back through the front gate. Denver took one look at it and said, 'It's artificial lawn.'

'Really? It can't be, it's so lifelike.'

I was hooked, Denver had pulled a blinder and I was in. Our new company Likalawn Ltd was born.

We spent the next few months doing further research on where was best to buy the product, even taking a memorable trip to China to visit a factory that manufactured the artificial lawn, where we were assured exporting to the UK would not be a problem.

We had flown business class with BA from Heathrow to Beijing, a ten-hour non-stop flight. Not sure Denver had flown business class before, but for me, any flight over five hours you have to turn left when you board the plane.

We had booked to stay in the Hyatt hotel, central Beijing and spent our first full day sightseeing.

One of the things I was keen to see was the famous Tiananmen Square. I will always recall the horrific scenes of 1989, known to us Westerners as the Tiananmen Square Massacre.

We had no idea where it was but felt sure it must be within walking distance from our hotel. After walking around for about ten minutes we began to ask locals for directions. The first ten or so people we asked had not even heard of it, which I thought very strange, but I now understand the Chinese government refuses to teach the history of the Tiananmen Square uprising. Students in Beijing steer away from discussing it, particularly to Westerners.

It's amazing we didn't get shot by the authorities, as I rather stupidly and naïvely was stopping people and saying, 'But you must know where the square is! You know, famous for the tank man?'

We eventually came across a couple of girls who knew exactly where we meant and offered to take us there. En route, they suggested we might like to try a traditional tea room where you could sample some Chinese tea.

I thought this was a great idea, although Denver wasn't so sure. Pulling rank, I persuaded Denver it would be a laugh, and anyway, what harm could come to us? We arrived at a small shop, and once inside we were escorted downstairs and then into a back room and encouraged to sit on the floor cross-legged. There was lots of bowing and smiling by our hosts and various teas in tiny little cups not much bigger than an egg cup which were constantly brought in for us to sample. I can tell you now it wasn't PG Tips.

After about twenty minutes of this even I was waking up to the fact it might be a con. Typical stupid tourist, they thought. We eventually managed to escape, but not before paying the bill. As it had been charged in the local currency, the Chinese yuan, I had no idea what we had been charged. It was only a couple of weeks later when my credit card bill arrived that I realised we had been fleeced. The bill, once converted to sterling, was just over £350. Now that's exorbitant for a cup of tea in my book. A solitary lesson learnt; I felt stupid. You would never think I was capable of running a successful business.

The following day Denver and I took an early morning flight from Beijing International Airport to Qingdao Airport, a flight that took over an hour and a half, so we turned right when we boarded.

We were met at the airport by the owners of the factory. On this occasion, the locals could not have been more hospitable. They not only met us at the airport, but once we arrived at their factory, which was only a ten-minute car ride away, we were introduced to some key employees and then given a guided tour. Later they arranged a light lunch, which I couldn't eat because it looked like a little sparrow had been cut in half and cooked over a candle. I just pushed the food around my plate.

We thanked our hosts profusely for their kind hospitality and we were then taken back to the airport for our return flight to Beijing.

It had certainly been a great education both from the point of view of getting a much better understanding of how artificial lawns are made, but also a great education in seeing the real side of China.

Once back in the UK I was able to email my contact at the factory and get some firm prices for the type and weight and length of the lawns we wanted to buy.

We never bought from this factory, but they did enable us to negotiate a very good rate from a local factory based in Kidderminster, which was once the carpet-making capital of the world.

In recent years, partly due to a change in fashion and the desire for wooden floors, they had hit on hard times. This company, now called TigerTurf, used to make carpets but had switched over to making artificial lawns a few years back having seen the potential growth in the market. Evidently, the process to make a lawn is very similar to making a carpet, and they were able to adapt the existing machinery to do the job.

We rented an office in Bromsgrove, just off Junction 4 of the M5. The office itself was small, just two rooms, a toilet and a tiny kitchen. When I say kitchen I mean a sink and a microwave – the essentials, you know?

The building was once part of an old milking shed. Memories of my time in Handsworth Wood came flooding back. The original farm and farmhouse were still in operation, but for many farmers, times were proving to be very difficult. They had, very sensibly, decided to rent out a few of their old outbuildings that were no longer needed for farming purposes. In addition to the office, we also had access to a couple of large metal shipping containers, which we could use to store the lawns and machinery as needed. The daughter of the farmer, a girl I still only know to this day as Piglet, worked as a stewardess for British Airways when BA used to be based at Birmingham Airport. She still lived on the farm albeit in one of the small cottages adjacent to the main farmhouse. I knew Piglet (a nickname she was given from work) because my then-girlfriend was also a stewardess for a while and she worked alongside Piglet on many a flight.

Small world.

In the unit across the yard were a couple of lads selling performance cars. It was a nice little niche business specialising in selling various top-of-the-range motors, but they particularly liked dealing in BMWs.

One lad was slightly older and appeared to be there full-time, so I would often see him when I would walk past making my way up to the shipping container, which was at the end of the farm outbuildings. His business partner had another full-time job working for a BMW dealership in Birmingham, hence their love of BMWs, but I had never met him.

One day I had spotted a BMW M3 that I liked. It had just come into their small showroom so I walked over for a closer look. As it happened, both lads were in that afternoon, so for the first time I was introduced to the other lad.

'Gary!' I said. 'I don't believe it, what are you doing here?' Gary was the husband of my PA, Tanya, at BXT.

Come on, these coincidences keep happening to me. I mean, I know it's a small world and all that, but it just feels... big somehow. Or bigger. I don't know. Dad, it's happened again!

# Chapter Thirty-six

It is a truth universally acknowledged that a man in possession of a small fortune must be in need of a wife.

Universally acknowledged, that's the bit that gets me. Universally acknowledged by whom?

Everyone except the man, I guess.

But it's a good point. I had been married, very happily married to BXT. Now that relationship had ended, and I was lonely. It doesn't matter how much money you have, what fantastic hotels you can afford to stay in or what exciting adventures you have; unless you can share it with someone it becomes meaningless.

Oh sure I'd had proper relationships, even long-term ones, but nothing that was ever this is it, this is the one. I'd been close, but something always held me back. Work mostly. But now I didn't have work. And I was single.

Filling my days was easy. I had Likalawn with Denver and a joy for travelling.

One of the best places I'd been to was New Zealand. It was wow! That's where I swam with dolphins, something I'd always wanted to do.

It was at Akaroa Main Wharf, on New Zealand's South Island, where I joined a group all heading to 'Swimming with Dolphins'. Once there, we checked in and then all changed into wetsuits and boarded a small boat to head out to sea searching for the dolphins.

The skipper obviously knew roughly where they might be and before long we were all jumping off the boat and into the sea. We had the sheer privilege of seeing these amazing creatures come up and swim alongside us. They were so close you could reach out and touch them. We were not allowed to touch them, that had been made very clear in the short safety briefing we had before we joined the boat. Quite right too, these are after all wild animals and we needed to appreciate that this was their territory.

After thirty minutes of swimming and hearing lots of oohs and aahs and laughter and giggles from my fellow swimmers, we were asked to get back on board, where hot chocolate and warm towels were waiting for us. Back onshore and after a quick hot shower, we said our goodbyes and made our way back to the car park, and that's when it hit me. All these strangers, who for a while had been comrades, returned to their cars. Some were hand in hand or had their arms around each other. Couples were chatting, laughing and recounting their shared experience. I was delighted for them but I felt so incredibly lonely.

I walked back to my car, alone with no one to share the wonderful experience, to relive it and recall it years later with family or friends. I sat in the car and cried. I knew then, more than ever, that life is for sharing.

Jane Austin, I guess you were right after all.

I'd hardly touched down when I sped to North Wales to see Diane's sister and brother-in-law. I'd kept in contact with them because I was godfather to their daughter, Siobhan. They'd asked me when I was still with Diane. It was such an honour and I felt so proud to have been asked, and I assured them that even if Diane and I split up, I'd still be a part of theirs and Siobhan's lives. It was a promise I was happy to keep.

At least once a year we'd meet up, and this little jaunt to see them had been arranged for some time.

'Nick, it's so great to see you!' Jane said, opening the door and embracing me warmly.

We chatted easily, the conversation dipping in and out of the now and the past.

At one point Jane announced, 'The spare room's all made up for you.'

I thanked her, although I hadn't intended to stay the night. But hey-ho, as usual it was turning into a fun night, and the last thing I wanted was to go home and be on my own.

It wasn't until after breakfast the following morning that I asked how Diane was doing.

'I thought you were never going to ask,' Jane said, grinning.

It turned out that Diane was keeping well but she had recently split up from her husband and was now living alone with her son Tom. There was no man on the scene. I said, all casual like, 'Feel free to pass on my phone number.'

It wasn't an hour later that my phone lit up with a number I didn't recognise. I was on the M6 and I hit the button on my steering wheel to take the call.

'Nick Terry,' I said.

'Hello, Nick Terry,' said a smiling voice.

I didn't need to ask who it was, I knew that voice. 'Hello stranger,' I said, grinning from ear to ear. Blimey, there were no flies on Jane. She must have been on the phone to Diane before I'd got to the bottom of their road.

It felt so good to be talking to her, maybe too good; approaching the intersection where the M6 splits with the toll road, I inadvertently took the paid route and thought, now there's someone up there marking my card. But I didn't care, it was just nice to be chatting with her.

After about ten minutes we both agreed there was too much to catch up on in a short call, so I did my gentlemanly bit and asked her out for dinner. 'Can you text me your address and I'll come and collect you?'

'Yes,' she said. And when it pinged through, I thought, she's only in Redditch? That's thirty minutes from my house!

We met up the following week, about four days after the call. When she opened the door to me she looked beautiful and sexy in a black skirt and red top, and I said, 'Hi,' and she said 'Hi,' back, and we both grinned.

I'd spent half an hour picking out my smart, casual outfit, and another half an hour picking out my car. Finally, I plumped for the Range Rover, thinking that turning up in my Ferrari would look like I was being flash or trying too hard. Her son, Tom, who was fifteen at the time, was staying around the corner at his friend's house while his mum was being taken out to dinner. They are very close – Mum and Tom, not the house!

She pointed out his little face peering as hard as he could out of the front window of his mate's house as we drove past. I think he was excited for her.

I had picked a restaurant in a place called Alcester, about fifteen minutes from Redditch. En route I said, 'Do you like Indian food?'

'Yes.'

'Oh good, because I've booked us a table at The Cellar. I think you'll like it.' If you want a romantic meal, The Cellar's the place to go.

Spinning to look at me, she said, 'Oh no, we can't. My ex-husband eats there!'

Ah!

Plan B was a nice little not-quite-so-romantic Indian restaurant in the opposite direction.

Seated and both employing our very best table manners, we talked and laughed until we were the last to leave, and then we talked and laughed some more on the way back to hers. She had left the bank a few years ago and was now a community nurse for the NHS. She'd been married, divorced, and had one son who she loved and was a really good kid.

'You can come in for a coffee if you like, but only if you park the car down the road and not outside, so Tom doesn't know.'

'Nothing changes,' I said. 'We used to do that the last time I saw you, only then it was your parents we were hiding from.'

Inside, she made the coffee and I took her in my arms and kissed her. I hadn't kissed her in close to thirty years, and all of a sudden I was nineteen again, with dreams of building a business empire, and Diane was a bird from the bank who walked past my office window after work each day that I'd fancied like crazy. It was a lovely feeling, but would it last?

# Chapter Thirty-seven

The relationship with Diane blossomed. It's amazing how different life can feel when you have someone special to share it with.

'I need to put you on my car insurance,' I said to Diane one day. We were sitting in my kitchen drinking tea and chatting. The night before we'd been out to a super restaurant and had been enjoying a meal with a bottle of red, only Diane doesn't drink much and I was driving, so we had to leave most of it there on the table. To be honest I don't drink much either, but sometimes it's just so nice to kick back and relax over lovely food and wine, and the previous night had been one of those occasions and I felt a bit short-changed. So, I thought, wouldn't it be nice on the occasional nights like that, that Diane could drive home.

'Can I drive your Ferrari?' she said, a twinkle in her eye.

I arched a brow and grinned. 'Dream on. No, for the Range Rover.'

Sipping some more tea she said, 'Okay.'

'Have you ever had an accident?'

She rolled her eyes.

'What?'

'You know I have.'

Wait a minute. 'I do?'

'Nick!'

I placed my mug back on the table. 'I don't know what you're talking about.'

'Oh you can be so infuriating sometimes.'

While I don't doubt that, I couldn't work out what on earth she was talking about.

Sighing, she said, 'You know I have, because I hit one of your vans.'

My face did one of those shocked 'Are you kidding me!' things where the eyebrows ping up into the hairline, mouth pops open and eyes go the size of dinner plates. 'When was this? What? Really?' I stammered.

Nearly all my company vans were sign-written with the company name and logo emblazoned on the side. A few vans, at the request of one particular client, had to remain plain. This was for security reasons, although I would have preferred to have all my vans sign-written because it was good publicity. In order to secure this particular business, I needed to adhere to the client's request and ensure all their deliveries were carried out discreetly in plain white vans.

One of my drivers working on that contract was a chap called Robert, and as Diane told me the story, it sparked a memory of the incident because he'd called to say that someone had skidded into his van.

Thankfully we didn't have too many prangs, and on that occasion, I was just pleased it wasn't my driver's fault, as he was at home eating his breakfast looking out of the window and saw a car slowly skidding on the ice outside. The car was unable to stop and the driver was unable to even steer the car. It bumped our van, which was parked on his drive, and then came to an abrupt stop. The driver wasn't hurt but both the car and van would need to be recovered by a tow truck and taken to a garage for repairs.

As she told it, I remembered the story because my immediate thought back then had been where could I find a plain van at such short notice. We always had a couple of spare vans in the yard, mainly because a driver might be off work, sick or on holiday. Naturally, all these vans had BXT written on the side. In the end, Robert, who had made it into the office, was told to use my car, which was a Jaguar XJ6.

Taking the keys to the Jag and looking more than a little happy at the outcome, Robert said he felt sorry for the young girl who was driving because she had explained to him that she was on jury service that day and was running a little late.

'That was you?' I exclaimed.

She didn't know that one of my drivers lived at the top of her street and she obviously only found that out because insurance details had been swapped.

My company vehicle insurance carried an excess of £500 in those days, so any minor work to repair a vehicle would not go through our insurance and instead the vehicle would go straight off to be repaired at a local garage we used in Selly Oak called Faulkner and Sons. This was run by the late Tony Faulkner and his two boys. Sometimes waiting for the third-party insurance company to give the go-ahead could take a couple of weeks. It was quicker, easier, and more cost-effective just to pay for the repair ourselves. Diane had to sort her own insurance claim out, and therefore from my point of view, there was no paperwork, and no link to Diane.

'So you hit my van, damaging company property I might add, because you were late for jury service and rushing, driving too fast in unsafe conditions,' I teased.

'Bloody cheek! I was not rushing!'

She was.

It seemed so funny to me that of all the vehicles she could have bumped into, it had to be one of mine. And then I thought, of course it did. My life revolves around coincidences; of course it had to be one of my vans.

Giving her a kiss and a hug, I told her I was running late, grabbed my keys and rushed out.

Being retired from BXT you'd think I had all the time in the world to be with the woman I loved, but life was busy. I spent most days at the Likalawn office trying to drum up business and keep the books straight. Denver was still working full-time in his sales role at ITV, based in Gas Street, Birmingham. We both felt that our new fledgling business could not at this stage afford to pay its two directors any salaries. Although Denver did not attend much in the week, he certainly pulled his weight when we installed the lawns, which tended to be at weekends.

One of the things we realised early on was that any potential client might want to see a job that we had previously done, a bit like when Denver was pretending to be a potential client.

As Diane lived in Redditch, we thought it was a good central location to have a show garden, which as a nice benefit also gave Diane a free lawn. After it was fitted and looking splendid, we used it to take some nice photos for our sales brochure and website. Diane's dog, Alf, took centre stage in the middle of the prestigious lawn.

Business came in from lots of different angles; even Denver's old boss from his days at Barclays Mercantile got in on the act.

The two were chatting about this and that, Denver telling him about his full-time role at ITV and his new business venture in artificial lawns. His ex-boss was extremely interested, and as luck would have it, he was thinking of having an artificial lawn put down at his own house. Like most of our early clients, he asked if we had a show garden.

'We have,' Denver said happily. 'We've got one in Redditch.'

'Really? I used to live in Redditch,' he said, 'so I know that area well. What's the address?'

Denver gave Diane's address and asked him if he knew where it was.

'Know it?' he said. 'I used to live there! That's my old house.'

Of course it was. I think I'm going to need a bigger book, Dad!

With business going well, we soon needed to order another five large rolls of lawn from the company in Kidderminster. The order was placed and paid for. There were no credit lines in those early days and arrangements were made for our new stock of turf to be delivered at ten thirty the following Monday.

Normally I wouldn't get to the office much before eleven most days as the company was, while doing well, still very much in its early stages and certainly did not need me to be there from the crack of dawn. However, on this particular Monday, I left my home in Worcester a little earlier as I wanted to be there in plenty of time to accept the delivery. Forever the punctual courier.

Just before ten that morning, and still a good few miles from the office, my mobile phone rang. It was my contact at TigerTurf to say that the driver had arrived at my premises but no one was there. 'Well no, the driver is half an hour earlier than we agreed,' I said irritably, adding, 'But please ask him to hang on.'

My leisurely drive to work that morning suddenly became a little more frantic as I sped up to get to the office as quickly as I could before the driver left in a huff.

When I arrived I saw the lorry had parked outside the office, so I drew my car up and unwound my window, explaining that the turf needed to be dropped off in one of my shipping containers just around the corner, and suggested he follow me.

He was a grumpy git and was clearly annoyed with me for being late, despite the fact he was half an hour early!

Following me round to the containers, he got out of his cab and walked to the side of his lorry. He proceeded to unhook the numerous straps that were keeping my five rolls in place.

'Let me give you a hand,' I said. There had been many a day in my previous life that I had loaded and unloaded a lorry and I also had a little sympathy for this chap as I knew only too well what it's like sitting around waiting for people to turn up and ruining your well laid out plan for the day.

'No, you're all right, mate,' he said. 'I can manage, but thanks for the offer.'

'You sure? I used to be in the transport business, so I can appreciate hanging around can be frustrating at times.'

'Oh really. Who did you work for?'

'It was a company called BXT,' I replied.

He stopped, looked at me, and said, 'Bloody hell, I used to work for BXT. Wasn't it run by Nick Terry? Lucky bastard sold out to a big consortium. Not that I blame him, would have done the same meself.'

'Well yeah, not sure about the consortium bit, but I am the lucky bastard Nick Terry,' I said.

From enemy to best friend.

To be perfectly honest I didn't recognise him, although I did make out I sort of knew him, but you have to understand that if you employ nearly 200 staff, towards the end it was difficult to remember everyone. He explained he used to always deal with Matt and Terry, who were, at the time, my Birmingham branch manager and my general manager.

He did say he had a good experience working for BXT, but then he was offered a job working for TigerTurf as their driver. He now lived in Kidderminster and it was too good an opportunity to turn down, or as he put it, 'It was a no-fucking-brainer!' Bless his little cottons.

But he did promise he would personally look after all my deliveries from TigerTurf from then on, and I was not to worry if I was running late again. I didn't correct him or explain I never run late, you were early.

Likalawn needed to hire vans from time to time so I went back to my old contacts from my days running BXT. At that time, I always used to hire from a company called Cartrux, whose managing director was a nice chap called Bernard. He remembered me and was able to give me a good deal on hiring vans, even though it was just the odd van here and there as opposed to hiring five or six a week.

We chatted a bit about old times, and he told me he was soon to be married to his long-time partner. 'Oh congratulations,' I said.

He smiled, looking very happy. 'We've been planning it for ages. Her work's super stressful and full-on, so we've had to juggle fitting it in.'

'What does she do?'

'She works for ITV.'

She worked on the desk opposite Denver.

Of course she did!

# Chapter Thirty-eight

One of the many things I loved sharing with Diane was Spain. After all the years of owning property out there I knew all the backstreet bars that sold the best tapas – the ones that normally only the Spanish know about – and the most beautiful tucked-away beaches.

The townhouse I bought from Dawson was great and definitely served its purpose as a short-term base. It was situated at the top of La Cala and was one of twenty-five small townhouses in a secure complex. It was deceiving when you approached it from the ground-floor level. It was actually three storeys high… well, in this case down.

We spruced it up without spending too much money and kept it for exactly twelve months before selling it and turning a nice little profit.

Just down the road from our townhouse, I saw a villa for sale at El Chaparral Golf Club. From the outside, it seemed it needed work, but its size and location looked perfect.

After a gorgeous lunch in a little taverna you wouldn't look twice at from the outside but I knew from experience sold calamari to die for, Diane and I contacted the estate agent and arranged a viewing. She explained that the lady selling the villa was not in the best of health. She also told us the vendor was an artist and a couple of her own pictures were hanging on the walls. The agent advised us to maybe coo a little about how wonderful they were. When I did see them, I genuinely liked them. I was into my art by then.

The couple selling were delightful, Eva Bako-Bittner and her husband Deivid. This had been their family holiday home for thirty years but their children had all grown up. Neither of them was in the best of health and they were now finding it hard to make the journey from Germany.

When we came out the agent asked what we thought.

'It certainly has potential,' I said. 'But I need to have a think about this one.'

I left it at that and we promised to let the agent have a final decision in a few days. In the meantime, I thought I should take a look around Mijas golf course, where I had first bought not only the apartment at Puebla Aida, but a few years later my first villa. It was an area I knew well and really liked, and before committing to buying the villa I had just seen in El Chaparral, I wanted, at least in my own mind, to be sure I had explored all options.

Diane flew back the following morning, so I was doing this recce on my own.

Before I knew it, I had arrived outside the villa I used to own on Calle Valencia, perhaps subconsciously drawn to it. I pulled up outside new and rather impressive gates. I could see that whoever owned it had spent some money.

Just as I was about to pull away, a car pulled in behind me blocking me in. I guessed it was the new owner, although it was not the gentleman I had sold to.

Stepping out of my car, I walked over to him to apologise profusely for being nosy.

He just laughed.

'Would you like to come inside and take a look?' he said.

'Really? Are you sure, I would hate to put you out?'

'Sure I'm sure. How long ago did you sell it?' he asked, unlocking the gates and swinging them back.

I told him and we both climbed into our cars and drove inside.

The front door was opened by a very attractive lady he introduced as his wife, Kelly. 'And I'm Gerry,' he added.

Inside, I was stunned. No wonder they were keen for me to see it, the transformation from when I had it was staggering. They had turned a nice villa into something straight out of Ideal Home magazine.

'My girlfriend Diane would love to see this,' I said, stepping into the master bedroom that just took your breath away.

'Bring her round,' Kelly said.

'She's back in the UK, flew back yesterday. But if you're sure, I bet when I tell her she'll come straight back.'

She did. Within forty-eight hours of my first visit I was back at Kelly's villa with Diane by my side. I knew Diane would love it too, and Kelly kindly gave us the name of the builder and interior designer. I half thought it might be Elona, but it turned out to be a builder called Dan and his partner Kate, who was the interior designer.

With the images of the villa fresh in our minds, we arranged to see Eva's place again, this time bringing along our new builder and designer team of Dan and Kate.

Three days later and we had a plan and a budget to make it look like Kelly's villa. It became a standing joke, because Dan and Kate kept asking us what sort of things we wanted to add or change over and above the designs they had presented to us. We would always reply, 'Just make it look like Kelly's villa.'

The deal was done and we bought Eva's villa. Perhaps I should have called it Kelly Two, but we actually gave it the name of Villa Un Vida – One Life.

The day I collected the keys for Villa Un Vida I had to go to the notary, accompanied by Jose of course. This is customary in Spain. The buyers and sellers normally meet at the notary office unless you have given power of attorney to your lawyer.

We met in his small office in the centre of Fuengirola and waited to be called in. While waiting, Eva whispered in my ear, 'I think you might be upset with me,' she said.

'Why, what have you done, Eva?' I said this as a joke, as I'm sure this little frail lady could not do anything wrong even if she wanted to.

'We have left the property in a bit of a state.'

Bless her, I thought. She was probably worrying because she had left a few personal items that couldn't get shipped back to Germany. 'It will be fine,' I reassured her. 'Please don't worry.'

After the transaction was concluded, Jose passed me a set of keys and we said our goodbyes to Eva and Deivid. We knew we were unlikely to see this lovely couple ever again, and we headed to see what awaited us inside our new villa

Without any exaggeration I can tell you Eva and her husband had left everything, and when I say everything, I do mean everything. It was as though they had just popped out to the shops and were about to return any minute. All the furniture was there; we were expecting that. Amazingly, they left books, bedclothes, all their clothes, CDs, paintings, cups, plates, food in the cupboard, food in the bins, washing in the washing-up bowl, and I even found their wedding album! I managed to get it returned to them via the agent.

They must have walked out and shut the door with passports in hand and the clothes they were wearing. I guess it was all too much for them to say goodbye to their family house, which must have held so many happy memories for so long. How sad. They were such a lovely couple too.

I found out through the agent who sold us the property that Eva passed away about two weeks later; she had cancer.

We started to clear out everything that had been left that we didn't want. The books, although lovely, were all in German, so they were taken to various charity shops along with their clothes. The bigger pieces of furniture that we didn't want we arranged to be collected by a guy who did house clearings, and it wasn't long before we had got on top of things.

Diane started clearing out the underground garage which Eva had used as her studio. A few of her paintings were still hanging on the walls and I took a closer look. I thought they were lovely. I turned to the bookcase to clear out the second batch of books and that's where I came across their wedding album. Alongside it was an album full of cuttings about all the places Eva had exhibited her artwork. Even more surprising was a catalogue from one of the exhibitions she had held in Dubai, which showed the prices of some of her work, together with a photograph of Eva standing next to a rather rich-looking sheik.

Hang on a minute, I thought, Eva is more famous than I thought. How modest of her. I ran downstairs to the garage where Diane was just tearing up another of Eva's old canvas paintings. 'Stop!' I shouted. 'These could be worth some money.'

Thankfully only a couple of works of art had been destroyed. The vast majority, about twenty-five pieces, were still safe in her large artist holdall.

Perhaps that bit of luck I used to have when running my company was still with me.

We arranged to have a few of the pieces of her art sent away to be framed, and they now take pride of place in a number of our rooms, a tribute to dear Eva. The remainder still sit in her holdall; I don't have the heart to sell them.

Before any work could start on the refurbishment of the villa, I needed to get some security fitted such as alarms and cameras. I contacted a local alarm company called Tecny-Ges, and the following morning their representative turned up. Thankfully, Jaime spoke perfect English.

Just as he walked through the front door I noticed another small plain black car pull up out front. Two men got out and one of them proceeded towards my own car, which I had parked half on the road and half on the pavement. He started to try the door handle.

'Hey, what you think you're doing?' I shouted.

Both men turned to look, then started walking towards me. The taller chap, who was about thirty and looked mean, said, 'Are you Nicholas Terry?'

A little unsettled, I said, 'Err, yes.'

'We're from the police,' he said, showing me his warrant card.

'Oh, thank goodness for that, I thought you were nicking my car.'

My immediate thought was they were going to tell me off about how I had parked my car, but then Jaime had also parked his car half on and half off the pavement so I wasn't sure that could be it. They looked too scary to be your basic traffic cops.

I was asked to go and get my passport, and while I was gone I could hear the two of them talking in Spanish. Passing Jaime, who was watching and listening with great amusement, I said, 'What's going on?'

'They think you've sold a property that you don't own.'

Right, that's not a good start. One of the policeman could speak English and said, 'We need you to come with us to the station.'

# Chapter Thirty-nine

Now hang on a minute,' I said, waking up to the seriousness of it all. I'm no angel, but I've never been in the back of a police car before, never been invited down to the station to help with their enquiries, never been arrested. The thought of it happening in a country where I didn't even speak the language, or not much of it anyway, was very sobering. 'Before we go anywhere, I need to talk to my lawyer.'

Before they could answer I was on the phone to Jose. Thankfully, over the years we have become good friends, so I had his private mobile number. Stammering, I explained the situation.

Jose asked if he could speak to one of the officers, and I handed the taller one my phone. After a few minutes the phone was passed back to me and Jose explained, very calmly, that someone called Nicholas Terry recently sold a villa in Mijas, a small village five miles inland from the coast. Only it was not his to sell. The new owners found this out when the real owner turned up one day and asked them what the hell they were doing in his villa.

Jose suggested to them that rather than take me to the police station for questioning, they should take me to the notary's office in Fuengirola. The judge could confirm if he remembered me as being the chap who had fraudulently sold the property. Jose agreed to meet me there. Good old Jose, what would I do without him?

He and I were one hundred per cent sure the notary would not recognise me. I apologised to Jaime, the alarm man, and told him we would have to rearrange. With that, I locked up my villa and got in the rear of the police car. No blue lights, no drama, it was after all just a plain unmarked, rather old and smelly Vauxhall Corsa.

While in the back of the car I telephoned Diane, who had gone down to the gym. 'Now I don't want you to panic,' I said. 'Everything is fine, but I am in the back of a police car being driven to see a judge in Fuengirola.'

That got her attention. I explained quickly what was happening and promised to let her know once this little fiasco was all over. I was meant to be picking her up from the gym, so I was hoping this wouldn't take long.

As we arrived at the notary's office, I saw Jose had also just arrived. He spoke briefly to the policemen in Spanish and one of them told the receptionist we were all here to see the judge. Thankfully, within two minutes he walked in from a side room. I gave him my best smile and said rather nervously, 'Hello.'

He looked, smiled back, turned to the policeman and shook his head. Phew!

The police apologised and even agreed to take me back via the gym so I could pick Diane up en route.

Jose later explained that it was all a coincidence that the fraudster either had the same name or at least used the name Nicholas Terry. The police had been notified that a 'Nicholas Terry' had just bought a villa in El Chaparral and they thought they had tracked him down. No such luck for the police I guess.

The story of my property ownership in Spain really does go full circle.

After the villa was refurbished to look like Kelly's, I invited the neighbours round for dinner, and of course to have a nose. Well, they had put up with all the noise and dust over the past six months so it was the least we could do.

Gary and Manya were from Birmingham; well, Manya was originally from Germany but had lived in Birmingham for twenty-five years, then Spain for the last ten. What is it about me having neighbours who lived in Birmingham? Anyway, they retired a few years back and were, so they told me, delighted to have new neighbours that would look after the property and not rent it out as a holiday home.

A few weeks later on another trip out, this time on my own, they returned the favour and invited me round to their place for dinner. Joining us was to be their daughter Jeanette and her partner Matthew, who now lived full-time in Spain.

Matthew was quite a character and we got on well. He invited me to join him and his friend for a game of golf at the nine-hole La Cala golf course, called La Noria. He played every Friday with John, who I instantly liked and have since become good friends with.

The owners of the golf course planned to expand it to an eighteen-hole and build various villas, townhouses, and commercial property around it. As yet it didn't have a clubhouse, but it did have a small café that housed the golf reception and shop. It was clear whoever was behind this set-up had a great vision for its future. To my surprise and delight, Matthew pointed in the direction of the 'big cheese' who owned the complex. I smiled to myself, stood up, walked straight over to him and said, 'Hello, Feliciano, does an ex-owner of one of your wonderful villas on Calle Valencia get a discount on membership here?' I think secretly Matthew and John were impressed that I knew the owner, or big cheese as we now referred to him – what a small world.

Friday morning golf became part of my routine. We would tend to book a tee-off time for around ten in the morning, and more often than not our three-ball was followed by another group of lads playing a four-ball. Matthew knew these guys as he tended to know everyone along this part of the coast. After we had finished, we would often share the same table with them for a beer back at the café. Our little three-ball soon became a seven-ball. This grew as people with holiday homes and friends in the group dropped in and out depending on when they were visiting Spain. Either Ian or Frank from our group was tasked with booking tee-off times for the following week. This would often involve us needing three tee-off times back to back to accommodate our burgeoning golfing party.

Frank was a smashing guy, and again like Matthew he knew a lot of people. He was a member of a walking group called the hash, nothing to do with drugs I hasten to say, and he was also a member of the classic car club. When Frank asked if I would like to join him as a guest one day on a rally, I jumped at the chance.

On the day of the rally I was introduced to Ian who ran the car club, and he kindly invited me to the next dinner and dance evening, which was to be held at El Chaparral Golf Club, a two-minute walk from my new villa.

Diane and I arrived and were introduced to a few people. When it came to going to the table, a nice couple called Jane and Gary asked if we would like to join them at their table of ten.

We discovered they were still UK based but recently retired and wanted to visit Spain as much as possible. Jane's father, who was president of a complex near to where they have their own property, was in his late seventies, and while he was still in good health, she did like to try and keep an eye on him as he lived alone.

I had got to know this side of Spain well, so I asked Jane, 'What's the name of the complex your father is president of?'

Looking up at me, she said, 'It's called Puebla Aida.'

Of course it was.

These coincidences were so frequent I kind of knew when one was about to happen. There was a feeling, like a change in temperature, and I thought to myself, 'It's going to happen again.'

When Jane was telling me about her father, it happened, and I knew it was going to link back to me somehow. I didn't know how, but I knew it would be there. I remember putting down my knife and fork and twisting towards her, suddenly becoming very attentive, using my eyes to urge on the story from her the way you might when someone's telling you a joke and mentally you're trying to beat them to the punchline. Then wham, there it was. Another coincidence, and another one for the book, Dad.

Later I told Diane about it. She shook her head. 'They always seem to happen to you. I never have anything like that happen to me.'

We were back in the villa getting ready for bed.

'I've had an idea,' I said.

She raised her eyebrows.

'Behave yourself, woman!' I chided, but we both laughed. There was a mirror in the bedroom, a full-length one. I was looking at my reflection. 'I'm going to be fifty soon,' I said, twisting so I could get a side view of my body. I wasn't fat, didn't have a belly, but even so, the evidence that I'd been on this planet for almost half a century was starting to show. 'Fifty,' I said, this time a little quieter.

'You don't look it,' she said.

I smiled.

'You look eighty,' she giggled.

I gave her a look that made her laugh even more. Then I turned back to the mirror. 'I'm thinking of having a party. A fiftieth bash. A big one. Friends, family, the works. What do you think?'

She was in bed by now and sat up. 'Yeah!'

So that's what we did. When we got home I sent out the invitations, booked a band, a DJ and caterers. It was to be held at home in the garden and a hundred people said they'd love to come along. That's when I decided to make it a charity event, see if we could raise some money for my favourite cause, Lucy's UK Donkey Foundation. The guest of honour, other than the birthday boy, was going to be Lucy herself.

The day of my birthday was hectic, with both Diane and me dashing about getting everything in place for the party. Before I knew it, people started arriving and there were kisses and handshakes and plenty of 'You're getting on a bit now, Nick!' and 'Welcome to the old and knackered club.'

I had a brilliant night catching up with old and new friends and family I hadn't seen in ages. At the appropriate moment, I nodded to the band and they fell silent. Mounting the steps to the stage, I picked up the microphone, every eye on me.

'What an amazing night!' I began, and everyone cheered. 'Okay, so we have the raffle…'

There were fifteen prizes that I handed out to grinning, happy faces.

'Can you believe we've raised over three thousand pounds tonight for the donkeys at Lucy's charity!' I'd asked that, rather than birthday gifts, everyone made a donation. The news that we'd raised so much money got the biggest cheer of the night so far, and Lucy blew me a kiss from the crowd.

I went on to thank everyone from the caterers to the band, the DJ, the serving waitresses and everyone attending.

Then I went quiet. Looked out. 'I need to thank one other person. Diane, will you join me on stage, please?'

She was at the front and we locked eyes. She looked bemused and slightly embarrassed. Handing her drink to the person standing next to her, she made her way up. As she did, I turned to face her, smiled, and went down on one knee.

Other than speaking to her son, Tom, just a few minutes before to ask him if he was okay with the idea of me asking his mum to marry me, I'd told no one what I was about to do. This was the biggest secret I'd ever kept. The gasp from everyone watching was audible. As I raised the mic to speak, some wag shouted out, 'Say no!'

The laugh that followed was big and joyous, and was perfect for the moment. When everyone fell silent again I looked at Diane, who had both hands cupped in front of her mouth, and said, 'Diane, will you marry me?'

# Chapter Forty

Fzzweeeefushhh! The rocket went up, up, up and exploded into the night sky in a thousand sparkly lights. I'd said to my buddy, 'When I nod at you, light the fireworks,' and he had.

Everyone at the fiftieth/surprise engagement bash looked up. Everyone except Diane, who was still looking at me, and whispered again, this time so only I could hear, 'Yes.'

So I'm fifty and I'm now engaged to be married. I have a fiancée. That's seems so funny to write. I didn't think I'd ever get married, but life has a way of knowing what you need even if you don't know it yourself, and even the most confirmed bachelor can only wake up so many times alone. Besides, you want to see Diane! I mean, I don't mind admitting I'm punching way above my weight. Okay, so that's the blokey stuff. Face value, pat on the back, fancy another pint, Nick? Comfortable, easy to chat about. Then there's the feelings that are harder to look at because they're so strong and I don't fully understand them all, and if I'm being totally honest here, they kind of scare me a little because of their power. The times when I look at Diane and she doesn't know I'm looking at her; the times when we're walking down the street and she reaches out to hold my hand; the times when we're driving, or flying, or just sitting together watching TV. The times when she smiles. The times when she cries. Even the times when she's mad. The times when she walks in from the gym all hot and sweaty. The times when she's swimming in Spain, or sunbathing, or sitting opposite me in a restaurant sipping wine. They're the times when I think: I love her.

'Congratulations!' I shook more hands on the night I got engaged than the Queen at an enthusiastic meet and greet, and I got patted on the back until I was bruised, but I didn't care.

A thought suddenly hit me, and I whizzed around searching the partygoers until I spotted him. Rushing over to Diane's son, I said, 'Tom, you sure you're okay with this?'

Grinning broadly, he said, 'Oh yes.'

Now, if you're going to get married, you might as well give it a little panache. A little style, you know? We're not kids, Diane and I, and this is Diane's second time, so we both felt a church wedding along with all that fuss wasn't what we wanted. Similarly, at a registry office you'd get caught up in inviting 'them' because otherwise they'd be upset, and then if you invite 'them' you'd have to invite 'them', and on it goes. No, not for us. However, the Cooke Islands, on a glorious sandy beach, dressed up, no shoes, just us and maybe one other couple, oh yeah, now we're talking. So that's what we booked.

The other couple had to be Jane and Kelvin, Diane's sister and brother-in-law, or Big Sis and Big Bro as they're known. He'd be my best man and she'd give Diane away. What could be more perfect?

We had a bit of business to take care of en route. Like I said, these things require some style, so we flew out to the jeweller in New York who'd designed Diane's engagement ring and agreed to make our wedding rings so they'd match, and we stayed the night at Trump Towers.

Trump Towers is over-the-top opulence, a bit gaudy, but utterly fabulous with it, and if you're going to New York it's the only place to stay. As it was our wedding trip, it felt only right to arrange for the hotel's limo to collect us from JFK airport.

Once we managed to get through security, which is always a slow process at any US airport, we collected our bags from the carousel and made our way to the arrivals hall. Waiting for us was a very smart man in uniform, wearing the obligatory chauffeur's hat and holding a plaque with our name on it.

'Good flight, Mr Terry?' he asked as I walked up to him.

'Yes, all good thanks. But we'll be glad to get to our hotel.' It was a night flight from Heathrow, so although it was only ten in the evening in New York, our body clocks were telling us it was three in the morning.

Even so, I'm always up for a bit of mischief, and I asked our driver if Mr Trump would be there in person to greet us at reception. I had forgotten that Americans, and in particular New Yorkers, just don't get our sense of humour. He had a real look of concern on his face when he replied earnestly, 'I'm sorry, Mr Terry, but Mr Trump won't be there to greet you, he just doesn't do that.'

Had I not been so tired I could have played him up something rotten, but I was far too tired so had to let it go.

New York's great fun. We did Macy's and caught a cab, 'Yo, have a nice day, now,' to Saks on Fifth Avenue, before making our way to the jewellers to collect the rings.

Next stop, Los Angeles, baby! We've got friends out there. Well, when I say we've got friends, we met them on a cruise ship the previous year. We had got on so well with this couple that we exchanged numbers and promised to stay in touch, adding, if you are ever in our country do look us up. I only add this bit in the story to warn you that, yes, we are that couple that do stay in touch, so don't ask us if you don't mean it!

We had a great time with Brian and Kathy and their delightful kids Chase and Dayna, who went to a lot of trouble to show us around and make sure we had fun.

Next stop… oh, where was it now? On the tip of my tongue… I got it! Our wedding. The Cooke Islands.

We had arrived on the Cooke Islands a couple of days before Kelvin and Jane, having booked a lovely villa on the beach. Kelvin and Jane had made their own arrangements and booked a smaller hotel just a little way along from us. I had already hired a car so we could meet them at the airport. The day before they were due to arrive, I thought I should do a quick recce of their hotel so I wouldn't get lost once they were in the back of the car. It's an old courier trick, check out the delivery address first!

We soon found their accommodation, but it wasn't a swanky hotel, in fact it wasn't even a hotel but a very old and tired log cabin stuck up the side of a hill, dark and damp. This was not good. I knew this wasn't good when Diane burst into tears, saying, 'They can't stop here, it's horrible.' Mmm, time for plan B.

We headed back down to the seafront and drove along until we found a fabulous hotel right on the sands. Of course, when we checked if they had any last-minute accommodation available, the only room they had left was a suite – of course it was. Anyway, I reserved the room in their name and settled the bill.

But how were we going to tell them without offending them?

Many years ago when we were all just kids really and I was dating Diane first time around, the four of us had taken a weekend trip to Blackpool. I know, I know, but it's what you do when you're in your early twenties. We hadn't booked ahead and instead decided that once we got to Blackpool we would just find a nice B&B.

We spotted what looked like a nice one, near to the fair, so went in. A nice chap invited us in to inspect the rooms. The smell of fresh paint hit me as soon as the door was opened, not a good start. We all proceeded upstairs, and once inside our bedroom, with the door half closed, I whispered to Diane that I hated it and we wouldn't be stopping there.

Once back out on the landing, Kelvin met my eye and asked, 'What do you think?' Diane just shook her head, and with deadly silence we made our way back down.

The nice man was still standing by the front door, and with great enthusiasm asked, 'So what do you think?' Adding as a kind of aside, 'Oh, sorry about the smell of paint, but we are freshening the old place up. Mind you, if I was you I wouldn't stop here, ha ha.'

That final sentence still makes us laugh today.

I took one look at him and said, 'Guess what? Sorry, but we're not.'

We waited like expectant parents for Kelvin and Jane to come through the small customs area of the Cooke Islands' one and only airport. 'There they are,' shouted Diane with excitement.

Despite my best efforts to hide behind a pillar to surprise them, Jane had spotted me and had also shouted to Kelvin, 'It's them.'

Once we were all in the car we headed off to what they thought was their accommodation.

Now for the tricky bit. 'Err, guys…' I said. 'We've been and had a quick look at the accommodation you've booked.'

Long pause.

I said, 'Now, do you remember many years ago when we were all in Blackpool?'

Another pause.

'Well, you're not staying there.'

Thankfully they laughed and were grateful we had managed to find them a hotel just a few hundred yards down from our place. In fact, their hotel was so lovely we have decided that when it's our ten-year anniversary we'll all return to the Cooke Islands and stay at their hotel.

That sorted, we settled down to the real business of the holiday, our wedding. Although we wanted it to be low-key, none of us could hide the excitement we felt.

The following morning after breakfast, Jane came down to our villa to get ready with Diane and I made my way to join Kelvin at his hotel. Despite all the shuttling around Dianne had managed to keep her dress a secret.

After a game of chess on a large outdoor chessboard, it was time for me to also get ready. I was in grey trousers and matching waistcoat with a white shirt underneath open at the neck, no shoes and a buttonhole in salmon and cream to match Diane's wedding bouquet. Looking at myself in the mirror I thought of all those years ago when I used to walk down to the bank to pay in the day's takings and hoping to get the pretty girl to serve me, and now here I was about to marry her. You could not have wiped the grin off my face if you'd slapped me with a cold fish.

We had arranged to get married on the beach, so I went down and stood waiting. The sun was high and warm, the waves gently lapping on the shore just a few feet away. Paradise.

When Diane walked out onto the sand to join me, I swear my heart stopped. She looked stunning. Her bridal gown was a full-length fit and flare sleeveless wedding dress in white with a sweetheart neckline overlaid with lace. She had diamond drop earrings and a diamanté headpiece. Her feather-cut blonde hair, coral pink lipstick and green eyes made her look like the most beautiful woman in the world.

Wow. And I get to marry her, I thought. Just… wow.

We said 'I do' and Jane cried for her sister and I laughed and we hugged and I don't think either of us have ever been that happy before or since. It was magical.

Once it was finished I invited my wife, 'Mrs Terry, may I escort you to your wedding breakfast over there in the restaurant?'

'You may, my husband.'

And we did. In all our finery we walked across the beach past the sunbathers and swimmers and deckchairs and towels, and you know what? Not one person said a word. So I shouted out, 'Guess what we've just done?' Nope, not a dickybird. They must all have been very British, but we laughed.

Sipping champagne and feeling like a million dollars, Diane suddenly looked across at me and said, 'You do realise when I first got married I became Mrs Knight? That's the same surname your mum had when she married Ralph Knight.'

'Oh yeah, that is a bit spooky,' I said.

'And your mum's birthday is the same as mine, twenty-seventh of May,' she added, 'and when Tom marries Ellis next year she will also become Mrs Knight.'

'Gosh, you're right.'

'But what's really spooky is that her birthday is also the twenty-seventh of May.'

I looked at Diane and said, 'You might have to start your own book.'

The rest of the day went all too quickly. Five days we spent together before Jane and Kelvin headed home via Singapore and Diane and I made our way to the airport to fly on to Australia.

'So,' Diane said in the back of the cab surrounded by our cases and bags, 'what's the chance of seeing Trevor and Susan at the airport?'

This was a standard joke whenever we went to an airport, as most of the time we did see them. Trevor and Susan lived close by in the UK and also had a home in Spain near our own. We also seemed to share the same itinerary, and after a few dozen times – I'm not kidding – spotting one another flying in or out on the same plane, we struck up a conversation and unwittingly have been waving to and greeting each other at the airport ever since.

Checking in, we looked, but no, there was no Trevor and Susan. Would have made a great story though.

We landed at Auckland, and while waiting for a connecting flight to Sydney, I spotted a familiar couple standing looking at the departures board.

'Hello,' I said. 'You two are a long way from home.'

Trevor turned to look at me. 'You have to be kidding me,' he said. Yep, it was Trevor and Susan. You couldn't make it up.

After Sydney, we flew back to New Zealand, where we hired a motorhome. It was nice to be back there, but this time to share the adventure (far better than being on my own with the dolphins!). We drove around the North Island for ten days, wild camping everywhere. Boy, I love that country.

We then flew back to the UK, stopping off in Dubai for five days before Mr and Mrs Terry, with shiny new wedding rings on their fingers, finally arrived back at Heathrow.

Now that's how you do a wedding in style.

# Chapter Forty-one

L ife for me has been very good.

Since I sold my business in 2003, I have attempted to keep a low profile and stay well under the radar. I invested the proceeds from the sale into a few rental properties and I live quietly off the income.

No financial stress, which is all I ever wanted. And the best luxury I have? Time. Time to go to Spain and be in my lovely villa in the sun, and time to be comfortable here in Worcestershire.

I had been living in an old manor house, called Abbey Manor, built around 1816 by the Rudge family. That sounds a bit grander than it actually was, as I was only living in a third of the house. About ten years earlier it had been split into three individual properties.

It was an attractive, big old house just on the outskirts of Evesham, a small market town in Worcestershire.

When the house was built by the Rudges, they excavated a large number of stone gargoyles from the site. Apparently, they had been buried by the monks from Evesham Abbey when Henry VIII decided to dissolve the monasteries between 1536–1541. All these unusual stone artefacts were dug up and placed in the manor house, which made it appear gothic and unique.

It had originally been the family home of the Rudge family, but it was also used by the Red Cross in the First World War as a hospital. The hospital continued for six years and treated more than 3,600 soldiers – none of whom died. It had also been a hotel, school and then lay empty and partly derelict for twenty years before being rescued and renovated circa 1995. This is when the manor house was split into three very distinct properties.

Within the thirty acres of grounds, which were shared by the residents of Abbey Manor, stands a large stone obelisk which the Rudge family had erected to mark the losses in the thirteenth century at the Battle of Evesham, officially known as the Leicester Tower but known locally as the leaning tower of Evesham.

The great battle had taken place in August 1265 within what is now the grounds of the manor. It is this spot where the Earl of Leicester, Simon de Montfort, who is credited with being the true founder of democracy, was slain by King Edward I, son of King Henry III.

Despite loving the house and its history, it was time to sell and move on again, but given this was such a unique property, I thought it would either sell quickly or hang around on the estate agent's books for months and months.

I arranged for local agents Hayman Joyce to place the property on the market, and a very likeable man from the agency called Martin assured me he thought it would sell rapidly. He was right, it sold within one week of going on the market to a chap called Alan, who was, at that time, living down in South East England having sold his business in Birmingham. He had retired to the South coast some twenty years previously after he sold his company, but now he felt it was time to be back near his family in the Midlands. He, like me when I first saw the house, fell in love with the property and decided there and then that it was the one for him.

I was away the day Alan came to view the property, but Martin had done an excellent job showing him around, not only the house, but the extended grounds. Alan had already sold his house, but unfortunately, it was to the government!

His house had been a compulsory purchase due to the fact it sat right in the way of the new HS2 train line. In one way it was good news because I knew he had definitely sold, and the buyer, good old UK plc, was not about to change their mind. The bad news was it took nearly twelve months for his sale to go through.

After the deal had all been agreed, thanks to Martin, Alan was keen to meet me and I guess to reassure me the sale would go through. The wait required patience, not my forte. However, he had paid £50,000 over the asking price so I wasn't too unhappy, and I was looking forward to meeting him.

So about a month after the sale had been agreed, Alan drove up from the south with his wife to meet me and take a more detailed look around. When they arrived at Abbey Manor, the very first thing he said to me as he got out of his car was, 'Hello, Nick, you don't remember me, do you?'

'Have we met before then?' I asked. He was right, I didn't recognise him or recall his name. 'I used to use your courier company,' he said.

He went on to explain that he had built up a company in Birmingham then sold it and retired down south. The name of the company he sold was Birmingham Race and Rally – the company my friend Kieran had bought – yet another one for the book.

After I moved out of Abbey Manor I bought a house with my new wife Diane in the village of Sedgeberrow, just outside Evesham – big mistake. Oh, just to be clear here, not being married to Diane, but the new house in Sedgeberrow, I hated it.

All my previous houses had character of some sort, but this one felt soulless to me. Don't get me wrong, it was a nice house from the point of view it was big, new and detached with four bedrooms, but to me, it was just a box.

Within twelve months I had decided I needed to move again. This was going to be my seventh move since buying my first house in Quinton and I was determined to make it my last. I registered with an online agency and submitted the style, number of bedrooms, area, price and type of house I was looking to buy.

A few weeks later I had an email pop into my inbox saying the system had found a house that fitted my criteria and I duly clicked on the link. Sure enough, it was exactly what I was looking for and I immediately tried to arrange a viewing.

The first problem I had was that I was in Cape Verde. I was, at it happens, flying back later that day, so I knew I could visit the property the next day if it was convenient for the vendors.

Unfortunately, the agents told me that there had been such a lot of interest in the property they were now restricting viewing to only those who were in a good position. Unless you had sold your house or were a cash buyer you couldn't even get to view the house.

With my fingers crossed and telling a little white lie, I did persuade the agents that I was in that position even though my own house at

Sedgeberrow wasn't even on the market. I could, I told them, if push came to shove, raise the funds to buy this house even if mine had not sold, and it was on that basis the agents allowed me to view.

The house was as nice as it looked in the photos so without hesitation I made an offer to pay the full asking price. I committed to exchanging contracts within four weeks as long as they gave me a completion date six months away. The house was a new build, built by the current owners a year previously, but for their own personal reasons, they needed to move. Thankfully my offer was accepted, partly because it was a fair offer and the six-month timescale also suited them. I think they agreed to sell to me for one other reason. The owner knew me.

The house was being sold by Martin, who had acted as an agent selling the manor house to Alan – what a small world; honestly, you couldn't make it up – another one for the book, Dad.

Time really is the best luxury to have, and best of all, I now have the time to spend with Diane and Bailey, my dog.

I live a happy, peaceful life. The dog, a cockapoo and still such a puppy, has added so much joy to my life. He really is a bundle of fun, and I guess, never having had any children of my own, he is as close as I will get to having a son.

In March 2020, I reached a real big birthday milestone, my sixtieth.

On my previous couple of biggies, my fortieth and fiftieth, I had tried to do something a bit memorable. For my fortieth I took a group of friends to Monte Carlo and for my fiftieth I had a big party at my house, ending up down on one knee and proposing to Diane.

For my sixtieth I was delighted to treat a few friends to a night out in Birmingham, staying at the Hyatt hotel on Broad Street and then going on to see Jimmy Carr, who was at the Symphony Hall, a one-minute walk over the bridge linked to the Hyatt. Afterwards, we all took a brief two-minute walk up Broad Street to a very nice Indian restaurant that I had booked. It certainly made me feel very old walking up Broad Street seeing the young revellers out enjoying themselves on a Saturday night – don't these girls feel the cold!?

Only three days after this celebration the country went into the first lockdown. My bash must have been one of the last parties allowed.

Lockdown gave us all time to reflect, something I like to do anyway. I like to look back, I like to reminisce. That's when I decided to write this book and tell the story of my time at BXT and the incredible coincidences that have peppered my life. I guess I can't be the only seventeen-year-old who has dreamed of becoming a millionaire and wondered what that lifestyle might be like, so I decided to kiss and tell. If you take nothing else from this book, know that it can be done. Don't let anyone tell you otherwise.

If you would indulge me and allow me to pass on one nugget of wisdom from my time in business it would be: think beyond the obvious. As we used to say back in the day, 'BXT, more than just a courier.'

It was September 2021 and the weather forecast was set to be good for the next few days, so last minute I booked a campsite over in mid Wales. One of the best things about retirement is you can do things on the spur of the moment.

Having arrived at a lovely site which was next to both the River Severn and the Shropshire Union Canal, which is great for walking the dog, Diane and I spent a couple of days relaxing, or what I like to call busy doing nothing.

However, by day three I felt the need to go and explore. Barmouth was only a forty-minute drive from our site, and as this was one of the places Diane and I used to visit when we first dated back in the early eighties, we thought it might be nice to revisit the place and see if it had changed much.

As we approached the centre of Barmouth, I pointed out the very bed and breakfast we had stayed at all those years ago. I do have an amazing knack that if I have been to somewhere once, doesn't matter how long ago or where it is, I can normally find it again straight away, which was a very handy skill to have as a courier.

I was also telling tales about how I used to come to Barmouth on my motorbike with my good friend Dave Fortune, and I pointed out to her the various pubs we used to visit as teenagers.

It was Dave who got me into the courier racket, getting me my first job at Despatch Riders after he'd been there a couple of weeks himself. If he hadn't done that, goodness knows how my life would have panned out.

We had great times together, Dave and I. We used to get up early on Saturday morning and clamber on our 250cc Suzuki motorbikes and head down for a lazy day on the beach. Twelve hours later, normally after a fish and chip supper, we would head back home. Happy times and happy memories.

With Bailey attached to his lead, we crossed the road and stood on the pavement looking out at the beach and the sea beyond. It was a gorgeous sunny day, really warm for late September and the beach was bigger and sandier than I remember. It was also rather quiet.

'I wonder if dogs are allowed on the beach?' Diane said.

Looking around for someone to ask, I spotted a man and his dog walking towards us.

'Excuse me,' I said, 'are you local?'

He turned and said, 'No, sorry, mate.'

I was looking at his dog and Bailey saying hello to one another. We both were. Then I glanced up. 'Oh not to worry, I was just wondering if you knew if dogs were allowed on the…'

Oh my God!

OH MY GOD!

'Dave?'

'Nick? What the…'

I don't believe it. Turning to my wife I said, 'Diane, I'd like you to meet my old friend Dave Fortune.'

I couldn't wait to tell Dad the story. So as soon as I could, I called him.

'Hi, Dad, how you doing? You are never going to believe what happened to me today.' I relayed the story, Dad listened, and there was a pause, and of course I knew what was coming.

True to form, Dad simply said:

'One for the book, son.'

# Want to Get Involved?

If you have an astonishing story of coincidence to share, please send it to:

## nick@authornickterry.com

The best stories will be shortlisted, and the successful writers will be contacted to see if they would like their story to appear in the next book -

### 'Another One for The Book'

Stories must be no longer than ten thousand words. Full terms and conditions will be sent to each participant prior to publication so please ensure you include your full contact details.

Your details will not be passed to any third party or used for any form of sales or marketing.

## You can also keep in touch by connecting online

www.authornickterry.com
www.oneforthebookson.com
www.bluepoppypublishing.co.uk
Facebook: @authornickterry
Facebook: @oneforthebookson
Twitter: @authornickterry
Twitter: @bluepoppypub
Instagram: @authornickterry

# A Request From the Publisher

Creative people thrive on praise. I once had the privilege of meeting Dame Judi Dench and I apologised before praising her acting skills saying that she is probably sick of hearing it. She was charming, of course, and confessed that you can never hear too much praise.

So, if you enjoyed this book, Blue Poppy Publishing would like to make a request on Nick's behalf.

Please take a moment to write a review; perhaps on the website where you bought the book, or on Goodreads, or anywhere really. Or just tell a friend.

It need not be long. It doesn't have to be all praise. The best reviews are genuine honest ones. We don't even mind if you want to be critical, although we do ask you, please, to be constructive.

Thank you.

Oliver Tooley

www.bluepoppypublishing.co.uk